Lau

CW00859094

/

Cathryn Pownall

Dedication

For my Mike, with love.

About The Author

Cathryn Pownall is an accomplished writer with a passion for storytelling. Her writing career spans several decades, during which she has written on a wide variety of topics, from personal experiences to motor racing, and even historical research.

One of her notable works is a blog that she wrote for six years, chronicling her journey with her husband's Alzheimer's disease. Her writing provided a platform for her to share her experience with her audience, creating a sense of community and awareness about the disease.

Pownall has also been working on a book about her father's birth, which has involved extensive research over the years. She is a dedicated and meticulous researcher who is passionate about sharing historical events and stories with her readers.

Pownall has also contributed to various motorsport magazines, writing articles on Formula Ford 2000 and producing her own small club-racing magazine. She later transitioned to writing about the EMRA motorbike-racing club, mainly as a supporter of one particular rider.

Currently, Pownall is a GCSE English and functional skills English teacher to adults, where she often writes articles and short stories to inspire her learners. She has also written short stories for her family as gifts, as well as poetry for her own enjoyment. With her vast experience and passion for writing, Pownall continues to make a positive impact on her readers and students alike.

Table of Contents

A visit to the urologist leads to a hilariously ironic Facebook post that many people "liked". That post became the spark that ignited the start of my blog, chronicling the comical happenings of our Alzheimer's journey.

Mike had already been living with Alzheimer's for three years when we decided to document our funny encounters for the enjoyment of others. Our first entry was the Facebook post that started it all.

So, join us on this journey filled with humour, tears, and joy. Sit back, relax, and enjoy our story.

The Pecking Order

7th January 2016

Mike decided today that he would like to be laid to rest with Honey's name tag.

I pointed out that Honey may not have finished with it, depending on how long we have before we have to deal with that sort of thing.

I went through the motions of being indignant that he wanted to rest for all eternity with his whippet rather than his wife, and we went on to discuss the crematorium in Nuneaton. In a macabre way, it's so lovely there for the mourners to be able to look out over the fields during the service.

Anyway, all this has been brought about by the urologist's blunt manner and insistence that there is no point in treating my husband's prostate cancer if he hasn't got 10 quality years left. He wants a prognosis from the psychiatrist who diagnosed Mike's Alzheimer's before he'll commit to anything.

Well, how long is a piece of string?

I was able to get the official medical terminology for this from my stepdaughter, Vicky, whose background is as a paramedic. She says the consultant is a twat, so we've got that one sorted.

I thought I may be able to write a daily blog, but working full time put paid to that idea. In fact, it was another two months before I wrote anything else.

Bottoms Up!
March 16, 2016

It's very important, when caring for somebody with Alzheimer's, that mealtimes are strictly adhered to and that they are nutritionally balanced, especially when a cocktail of tablets has to be administered at these times for them to be effective.

However, I walked into the kitchen today only to find Mike, perched with one cheek on a tall stool, halfway through a packet of fruit biscuits, his tablets ready to take, necking the remnants of a bottle of Muscatel!

I missed my vocation.

Mike and I could really see the funny side of the situation of him drinking wine straight from the bottle, and those early days were full of laughter.

However, Alzheimer's wasn't the only illness we had to deal with. Mike was seeing a urologist for his prostate cancer; an ophthalmologist for his traumatic glaucoma (from a squash ball in the eye many years previously); and a neurologist for his cluster headaches from which he had suffered excruciating head pain, periodically, for years. The psychiatrist was just another "ist" to add to his collection.

The Eyes Have It
26th March 2016

Well, this is a new one: eye casualty on a Saturday morning.

A week ago, Mike's right eye was very red. We just thought he'd got some hay or straw in it: he's a devil for throwing the hay around when he's filling the nets. However, it started to look yellowy, so I got the GP to have a look.

After a week of antibiotic eye drops, I thought it had settled down, even though he was complaining yesterday of it being sore. Ever the carer, I left it until bedtime before I had a proper look... Oh my word: there was a blister on his eyeball the size of half a pea! No wonder it was uncomfortable.

I instantly took a photo to add to the gallery, and I've brought him to eye casualty now.

When Mike had his successful glaucoma operation last year, a trabeculectomy, the consultant, Mr K, told us to come to the eye casualty if there were any problems with the eye. It's a shame I only remembered that this morning instead of last week. I'm now feeling guilty for not having brought him here when his eye was first red, and for having so much faith in antibiotics that I didn't take enough notice of the eye once the drops had been prescribed.

Rather than a carer, I'm more of a *couldn't-give-a-buggerer!*

Mind you, as always, Mike has made me laugh several times on the way here and whilst waiting. He always sees the funny side of things, and I love being out with him, albeit for a hospital visit.

All's well that ends well. The yellow last week was the start of conjunctivitis, which the antibiotic drops cured; the blister in the eye is the actual bleb put in by Mr K and his team. It's bigger now because the outer layer has become thinner, but it's doing its job perfectly and the pressure is 12, which I am led to believe is normal. Big sigh of relief.

I briefly mentioned the fact that Mike suffered for years from Cluster Headaches, a badly named condition also officially known as paroxysmal hemicrania, and more accurately called the suicide headache. The first time he had an attack was when he was about 58, and I thought he was having a brain haemorrhage and was dying, because he was rocking on his knees, holding a towel to his left eye, and screaming. This became a way of life that we had to manage. Luckily, Mike's attacks were episodic rather than chronic, but it was life-altering when he was in one of his cycles.

The following blog post involves a visit from "The Beast".

It's official: Mike's a vampire!

28ᵗʰ March 2016

It's definitely garlic!

I have suspected it for a while, but I'm now sure. Three years ago, I cut garlic from our diets because of my IBS, but didn't link it to my husband being pain-free from his cluster headaches during that time.

A year ago, Mike had 2 episodes of worrying "shadows" that luckily didn't develop into a full-blown cluster headache. Both of those times were after he had been out for a meal and chosen dishes that contained garlic. So, for the past year, we have been avoiding garlic in restaurants, and at friends' houses, just in case it wasn't just a coincidence.

Tonight, because I was short of time, I made a carbonara using a pot of Dolmio sauce. I didn't tell him that there was garlic listed low down in the ingredients. An hour after eating, Mike stood up to let the dogs out and was suddenly clutching his left eye and staggering. He said, "cluster", and collapsed on the settee.

Realising, I said, "Sh*t! You've had garlic," and rushed off for the Sumatriptan, which he used to take a lot but that I give him now infrequently if he has a "normal" headache with "shadows", usually if he has forgotten his daily medication. The drug seems to have beaten it off and he's sleeping soundly, and I'm hoping it will go away.

This has confirmed for me that garlic is a trigger for Mike, and I will never knowingly let him have it again.

Now that he has Alzheimer's, it would be devastating if the "beast" were to return.

I'm not convinced that his cluster headaches haven't been partly responsible for the dementia, although I have absolutely no scientific evidence to back this up...

_____

"The Beast" did indeed return but, in later years, Mike forgot the pain as soon as it finished. Before Alzheimer's, Mike would have what he referred to as "a hit", which was a jagged pain in the left eye that had us running for the Sumatriptin and led to anxiety that a full-blown attack was on its way. Mike was so tense about these hits that he may have inadvertently brought on an

attack. However, when Mike was in his last couple of years of Alzheimer's, he would have an attack that had him clutching his eye for a few seconds, but as soon as it was over and he had forgotten about it, he relaxed, thus reducing the threat of a full-on attack. Funny how these things pan out.

I never did give Mike garlic again, and I later discovered some other interesting responses to food.

Food For Thought
1ˢᵗ June 2016

Facebook has recently reminded me that it has been a year since I started Mike on his new super food diet, and I'm absolutely certain that it has made an enormous improvement in his cognitive health.

Let's not forget that, at the same time as starting this diet, he also started taking Mementine, an Alzheimer's medication, so his dramatic improvement could have been due to that. However, during the subsequent appointment at the Alzheimer's clinic, as I praised the tablet for having brought back my husband to me, the raised eyebrow and the humouring manner in which the psychiatrist said that she had never yet met such an extreme reaction, led me to believe that it was, in fact, the diet, coupled with the medication, that had improved Mike's brain function so greatly.

Personally, I didn't care what had caused the minor miracle. All I cared about was that I had my husband "back".

Breakfast is a great time to get the super foods into him. I serve his porridge with a great big spoonful of coconut oil. (I say a big spoonful, but that's only actually possible the first time you open the jar: after that, you have to keep it in the fridge, so every morning, you have to take an ice pick to it). Then I add dark red fruit, depending on what's in season. Mike loves black grapes best, although I'm told that blueberries are a better superfood and that blackberries are best of all. I use frozen fruits of the forest when we're out of fresh and, apart from needing a little sprinkle of sugar to counteract the sharpness, it's just as good. Finally, the porridge is topped by milled linseed, which is high in Omega 3.

Porridge is ideal for taking tablets with. Mike takes a cocktail of 9 tablets in the morning, and he finds it easier to swallow them with a spoonful of porridge than with water.

At lunchtime, savoury sandwiches and wraps can have sesame seeds added. Mike loves wraps, so he often has a sweet one for his pudding with a liberal spreading of Nutella. Linseed can be sprinkled on to add some brain food to the otherwise decadent pudding.

Whatever we have in the evening, I try to add turmeric. I started using it a couple of years ago and realised that it was doing wonders for my arthritis. It needs to be cooked but not overcooked, so it is easily stirred into casseroles, curries and soups, ten minutes before serving. The Turmeric Users' Group on Facebook has many more cooking ideas and the instructions on how to make "golden paste": worth a look.

Tinned fish, such as sardines and mackerel, is a good brain food but Mike really doesn't like fish, so I go overboard with the turmeric, red fruit, linseed, and coconut oil.

As I said before, the doctor was really sceptical when I told her that the Memantine had worked wonders, so the super foods must be contributing.

Looking back, I had had an extra "good" year with Mike, thanks to the diet and the Memantine, and I am extremely grateful for it.

A bit of a Boob-oo
5th June 2016

This isn't the usual topic you will find on an Alzheimer's advice blog; however, today, I had a few hours of panic while I tried to find out to whom Mike had accidentally sent a video of me... naked!

Mike has a smartphone. I often have to come to his rescue when he has clicked on an advert or a link for something, and he can't quite understand why he has a picture of Jim Carey "ageing badly," or of a donkey sanctuary in need of funds, when he is trying to read about Manchester United football club. I usually reach across the bed, hit the back button a couple of times, and delete the items that he shouldn't be looking at. He is then happy to carry on browsing.

When he tries to use his phone as a camera, that opens another can of worms, and he ends up with photographs of the ceiling, his eyebrows or his left knee. This is what I thought was happening today when I came out of the shower.

I sat on the bed and started to put on my bra. I heard: "Ooh, hello," and turned around to see that Mike had his phone on selfie mode, and that he had just caught sight of me in my undressed state. I leaned over to press the button, striking a pose with my husband, only to realise that it was a video. At which point, I said: "Oh, it's a video!" and reached over again to stop it from recording. I told him: "There, you can look at that any time you want while I'm at work," and continued to get dressed.

A few minutes later, I saw him fiddling with the phone, so I intervened. I looked for the video in the gallery, but it wasn't there. It was at this point that I started to panic.

Had he posted it on Facebook?

Had he sent it to one of our friends?

Were my boobs about to go viral?

I called in Fred, our 18-year-old son, to try and find out what had happened to the video as he has much more knowledge of smart phones than I do. Squinting at the phone (in case he saw something that would send him off screaming), he assured me that it wasn't anywhere to be seen, so I shouldn't worry about it.

Nevertheless, I posted on Mike's Facebook profile: "Have I sent anything to anyone in the last 10 minutes?"

Throughout all this, Mike was absolutely killing himself laughing at my chagrin! Intermittently he was apologising profusely, but, for the most part, he was in hysterics!

I then tried to calm down, and we went over to the field to sort out the animals. I felt a lot better after a good dollop of fresh air. However, when we sat down for a cup of tea, and I switched on my 4G, there was one word posted on my Facebook wall from our close friend, Andy...

Yes.

Well, my heart was thumping out of my chest as I left Andy messages to ring me. Talk about palpitations. I felt like I was about to take an exam; I was that nervous. The ratio of Mike's apologies to his hysteria was now greater and he was beginning to worry about me. I didn't want him to start blaming himself, so I told him: "In retrospect, I'll find this funny, just not today!"

Eventually, Andy did ring me and was able to put me out of my misery. His "yes" was unrelated to my blue video and he, having sensed my panic from my calls, texts, and posts, was worried that one of us was ill. He too saw the funny side of things when I explained and allayed my fears: he had not seen me posing in the all-together.

Phew!

But what did happen to the video? I await Hugh Heffner's call...

_____

Hugh Heffner never did call, thankfully, and we continued to enjoy life. However, there were still upsetting moments, although not as frequently as they later became.

Another Lost Key
19th June 2016

Sitting at the bottom of the stairs, crying, is not terribly supportive of Mike, especially since he has already gone over to the field to give me some "space," but I'm becoming aware that he is gradually becoming how he was before the Alzheimer's drugs and superfood diet brought him back to me in April 2015. What am I supposed to do this time?

This has all come on from another lost key. Even when Mike didn't have Alzheimer's, he was always bad with keys. In 1997 he actually chucked his keys in the middle of the river Seine, near its source, whilst we were heading for Grenoble. Obviously, this wasn't on purpose: we'd been driving for hours, and Mike made a spontaneous decision to pull in at a parking area where there was a bridge that crossed the river; he wanted to look at the fish.

By the time I had put on my trainers, Mike was down by the water, on the sloping bank, looking at the fish. As I crossed the bridge, I saw something black plop in the middle of the river. Looking quizzically towards Mike to see if he thought it was a big, black fish, I realised he was staring at me in horror, with his hands over his mouth.

"I've thrown my keys in the water," he said, in a state of shock.

"Why?" I asked, putting as many extra syllables into that one word as possible to show my utter disbelief at what he was telling me.

Apparently, his back had spasmed, and his feet had slipped at the same time. The unconscious body movements to steady himself led to both hands shooting up in the air, the one holding the car keys catapulting said keys up into a graceful arc and depositing them in the middle of the Seine.

It was icy cold and fast flowing, so we did what any responsible parents would do: we sent our 12-year-old son in to get them.

Goodness knows what the passing drivers thought when they saw Joe in the water that was turning him blue.

"Silly Eengleesh people, sweeming in zat icy watter," or some such comments.

The amazing thing is that Joe actually found the keys, in the deepest, coldest, quickest-flowing middle of the river Seine; even more amazing was the fact that the keys still worked to start the engine; but most amazing of all was that we managed not to actually kill our son! We wrapped him up in layers before hypothermia could set in and got the car nice and warm. It didn't take long, and Joe was elated: partly because he had succeeded in his task, but mainly because Mike had thrust a 20 franc note at him as soon as he came out of the water and told him he could spend it on whatever he liked.

So, where was I? Well, I'm still at the bottom of the stairs, but I'm more ready to go and deal with the lost key and Mike's progressing Alzheimer's. Reminiscing the good times seems to be a helpful coping mechanism for me.

And there were lots of good times to remember. Mike and I had a wonderful marriage and always felt very lucky to have found each other. Obviously, we argued and fell out like normal couples, but, on the whole, we were friends and really enjoyed each other's company. I had my Mike for thirty years and will always be grateful that I did.

Bin There

10th August 2016

It's not the end of the world, but it's mildly irritating when the bins are out, ready to be collected via the refuse collectors, full to the brim because our son, Fred, and his girlfriend, Renée, have been tidying the house in readiness for getting two kittens, and Mike brings the recycling bin back in before it's had a chance to be emptied. This means that I have a tall bin full of paper, plastic, cans and glass to dispose of myself before next week. Either that or I have to chuck stuff away that can be recycled, and that, obviously, would mean the end of the planet, and I'm just not into that.

I already have to label all the bins with instructions such as: "Put kitchen roll in here!" so that I don't have to keep getting dirty pieces of yuk out of the recycling bin. I also have Christmas wrapping tape covering all the microwave buttons that we don't need to use so that Mike is just left with the ones that he needs for heating wraps and porridge. I have the same tape on the cooker to show which of the rings is no longer to be used, although since I've done this, Mike hasn't done any cooking on the stove (perhaps I could take it off because it does look awful).

However, we have just had a few delightful days away visiting various relatives in Stroud, Clevedon and south Wales. Mike was really on form, and we were both able to enjoy ourselves immensely.

I'm also pleased that the people we visited, Mike's son James and his family, Mike's brother Ray and his family and my cousin Rita and her family, were able to see him when he was doing well. He had great fun reminiscing with Ray and Sue about the old days (before I was born) as his memories of this time are still as clear as a bell. He also enjoyed the grandchildren's performance of The Lion King, and playing fetch with Zelda, one of our Echo's litter.

In fact, the only problem Mike had was with getting lost: James and Ray both have three-story houses, and

Rita has a massive labyrinth bungalow, so finding the toilet, especially during the night, caused some fun and games. Luckily, I have the wonderful ability to go straight back to sleep when disturbed so I never mind having to get up and help at these times, as I love knowing I can snuggle back down to sleep. It's a gift!

Reflections – 2022

Excessive rubbish wasn't a big issue when I look back. It was a time when Mike could go outside on his own and complete household chores, albeit badly. I had absolutely no idea how awful things were going to get and that I would eventually reminisce fondly about Mike's gaffs.

One of these gaffs was when he inadvertently locked his daughter in our small porch. I say porch, but it's only a foot across and acts more like an airlock system to stop pets escaping when the front door is opened. The outer door is clear glass and is never locked, so that deliveries can be left in the dry if we're out.

However, one day, while Vicky was visiting her dad, Mike found the key to the outer door and locked it, unbeknown to her. It wasn't until later, when Mike was fast asleep and Vicky tried to leave that she found herself wedged between two doors, one that she had pulled shut behind her, and the other in front of her, mysteriously locked.

Being the practical type, once she had ascertained that her dad wasn't going to wake up and rescue her, Vicky decided that her only means of escape was via the porch window (like the door, only a foot away from the wall of the house, so a bit of a squeeze). This window does not open fully, which added to the fun, but Vicky managed to extricate herself through the gap, and climbed onto the wheelie bin in a bid for freedom, albeit bruised, scratched and covered in cobwebs.

Obviously, I couldn't get in when I got home from work, so had to go around to the back of the house. Mike was blissfully unaware of Vicky's traumatic experience (as was I at this point) and was astounded to find the porch door locked, it not having been him who locked it, of course.

Needless to say, once I located the key, hanging innocently on the key rack, I unlocked the door and hid it so that it couldn't happen again.

Soon after this episode, we had a motion sensor speaker fitted by the front door. I recorded my voice saying, "Mike, don't go outside," which usually stopped him, although after a while, he stopped recognising it as my voice and told it to, "Sod off!" but by then the door was permanently locked.

Having Kittens
20th October 2016

We always used to have cats. We had five at one time, then four, then three, then two and then just one, who died when she was twenty-two. The youngest one to die was fifteen. They all managed to die of old age, which is because we live at the end of a cul-de-sac, and back onto fields, so the likelihood of them getting run over is negligible.

When the last one, Gobbolina, (don't ask!) died, Mike decided we would not have any more cats. For years he wouldn't be shifted in his opinion that five dogs, two ponies, two goats and several chickens were enough (Really?) In fact, he agreed that we could foster children, yet still said no to getting kittens.

However, Alzheimer's meant that he could no longer remember why he was so adamant not to have cats so, when I suggested that we get a couple of kittens to train two of our whippets not to chase other people's cats, he no longer objected. The fact that I'd been ridiculously turned down for fostering because of his Alzheimer's may have had something to do with it. They said that because I was married and it has to be a joint decision, and because Mike couldn't do the training alongside me because of his Alzheimer's, I was not eligible to foster. But that's another story.

What I have found is that the kittens make Mike happy. When we talk about them to other people, he says that they are naughty and that they scratch him, but when he is with them, he laughs delightedly. I do love to hear him laugh.

Mike still has his humour, although, at times, it can be a little inappropriate, but most people don't mind. These days, he is more likely to laugh at obvious humour, such as Jim Royle saying: "My arse!" rather than the subtleties of clever wordplay or irony. That's probably the reason why he finds the kittens so amusing: their antics are very slapstick.

I told Renee that one of the kittens could be hers, long before we got them, and she has taken her role of "cat mother" to the extreme. She has an uncanny way of making me feel guilty when she wants to buy something for Pagan and Luna that I think is too expensive. For that reason, I believe I have spent more on these two scraps than I spent on all five of mine over the twenty years I had them, not including vets' bills, of course.

Since we have had the kittens, they have spent a fortnight at Renée's, and then a further week with her while we went on holiday. Poor Mike doesn't really understand where they live or to whom they belong, but as long as they keep him laughing, I'm glad we got them.

Animals are non-judgemental and ours gave Mike a bit of normality when his world started to behave strangely. No wonder animals are taken into care homes and hospitals to help the residents and patients. I certainly took the dogs in to see Mike once he was in a home and they were such a tonic.

Mike always loved New Year and celebrated with relish and lots of alcohol. I was always the designated driver so that he could really let his hair down. January tends to get me feeling older and not any wiser, and 2017 was no different.

Happy New Year
17th January 2017

I haven't written an entry for a long time, and that is partly because I've been too busy, and partly because it's getting more and more difficult to find things to laugh about. Now that I'm back at work after the Christmas break, and our son, Fred, has gone back to university, the reality of the fact that Mike sometimes can't be left on his own is beginning to sink in.

Before Christmas, my idle thoughts were about where we were going to have Christmas dinner; what I would buy for my granddaughter, Maisie and my grandson, Ben; how I could make Fred's boring but necessary presents seem exciting. Now my thoughts are around day care; carers; au pairs. I had suspected that Mike would need more supervision before Christmas, but I was rushing towards the festive period with such fervour, that I didn't stop to consider how bad things were getting. It was almost as if Christmas was going to "solve" things; to provide all the answers; to cure Alzheimer's. Pretending that things aren't happening is one of my coping strategies. It's almost as if not saying it aloud, or not writing it down, means it's not true.

But it is true.

My maudlin demeanour has been exacerbated by the audio book I'm listening to in the car on the way to and from work. It's called Elizabeth is Missing by Emma Healey, and the protagonist has dementia. It's breaking my heart.

I've not made any new year's resolutions this year; I never keep them anyway. I have decided just to see what life throws at us and to meet it head on. What more can I do?

Let's hope we can still find things to laugh about in 2017. Happy New Year to all x

---

Thankfully, my mood did pick up, and I continued to research the possibility of getting an au pair to stay with Mike while I was at work. At this point, all he needed was company as he could still function on his own, although I was never sure with what I was going to be met when I got home...

Give a Dog a Bad Name

22nd January 2017

Mike has been making me some very interesting hot drinks just recently; I've had tea with milk and sugar, even though I don't take sugar; peppermint tea with milk, even though I don't like it with milk; plain hot water, even though I prefer it with tea; and normal tea that appears to be okay until I find the bottom is full of tea leaves. He dished up a "cup of tea" the other day in a glass: it was piping hot and smelt decidedly of strong liquor (presumably Amaretto, since that is his preferred tipple currently) and, as far as Mike was concerned, he had given me a cup of tea

Therefore, when I went into the kitchen last week, I was disappointed, but not surprised, to see almost a whole box of peppermint tea bags on the work surface: some had been ripped open and partially emptied, some were completely empty, and some were in the sink. Obviously, the work surface and the floor were mossy with green tea leaves.

I sighed and started to clear up, but then I discovered something extremely odd: the damaged tea bags weren't just ripped... some had claw marks!

Feline claw marks!

It's easy to jump to conclusions, and to blame Mike for everything that goes missing or gets broken. To be fair, it usually is him. I had even felt guilty when I told my stepson, James, that his dad wouldn't be able to make him a cup of tea when he visited from Stroud yesterday with his wife, Hayley, and the children.

Then today, without a kitten in sight, I found him making tea. There was a pile of wet tea bags on a plastic lid, and another pile in a dish. He was avidly stirring others with a spoon in the tea caddy.

"How many have you got in there?" I asked him, peering into the steaming caddy.

"Two," he replied.

"Shall we count them?" I asked, gently taking the teaspoon from him. "One, two, three, four, five, six."

"How many did I say?"

"Two," I informed him, salvaging a couple of the bags to make a cup of tea for me, before emptying the sludgy, black contents of the caddy down the sink.

I made Mike a cappuccino and we had a good giggle and a hug. As long as we can both still find humour in these situations, we can live to fight another day.

I am lucky that Mike does see lots of humour in many things, although not always appropriately.

I was pleased when I came home the other night from work and found him laughing at the television. He continued to laugh loudly while I cooked dinner.

However, when I went into the lounge, I found that the hilarious programme that he was watching was in fact "Unforgotten", a harrowing crime thriller about a murdered body in a suitcase.

He told me it was Monty Python!

I do love to hear him laugh, even if he has misunderstood the serious acting to be tongue-in-cheek irony. I just want him to be happy.

Anyway, I'm off to buy teabags!

Reflections – 2022

When living with Alzheimer's, there is a lot of looking back. In other situations, past mistakes can be learned from, and actions improved but, with dementia, the newfound strategies can no longer be applied as the sufferer has moved on and produced another, completely different, set of problems to deal with. Of course, these strategies can be used on someone else who is not so far into their journey, which is what I am trying to do with this book, but my knowledge and understanding of Mike's condition was always running to catch up with reality.

The Signs Were There
16th March 2017

The early signs of Alzheimer's are blindingly obvious and unmissable.

In retrospect.

In reality, the signs just go unnoticed until the diagnosis, when, all of a sudden, those early signs become blatantly clear, leading to pennies dropping, guilt manifesting and life changing.

Forever.

I remember lots of events, leading up to Mike's diagnosis, that were either funny, mind-boggling or irritating. Let me give you an example that includes all three of these reactions.

Friday evenings used to be spent at our friends' house playing a French card game, akin in complexity to Bridge. It's called Tarot but it's nothing to do with telling the future: it's a game using oversized cards, including the usual 52 from a standard pack, but which also comprises an extra face card (the cavalier) and a set of 21 trumps. Suffice it to say that it takes some concentration to follow the cards, spot your hidden enemy or partner and to win each hand, if you have predicted you will do so.

We enjoyed the game immensely and became more skilled as time went on. However, there became times when I felt that Mike was making a bad call, playing badly or just being daft. If I profited from it, great. If not, I would nag. But whatever the outcome, we all had a really good laugh, usually at Mike's expense.

In time, we started to play Uno instead, deciding that on Friday night, after a week at work, Tarot was too tiring for Mike. Even so, the hilarity still continued at Mike's gaffs and confusion.

Looking back, it was so obvious; why didn't we realise?

The first time I wondered if there was something more sinister afoot, was when we were mending the back fence, to stop our puppies getting into next door's garden.

I had seen that the garden centre (within walking distance) had some inexpensive fence panels. We pieced together enough bits of old panels that we would only need to buy one new one. I grabbed my purse to nip up and buy it, but Mike wanted to measure it all again to make sure. I humoured him to start with; after all, he was the engineer. But it soon became clear that he was confused as to where the new panel would fit.

In my usual placid and patient tone, I reiterated, whilst gesticulating, that: "That panel will go there and the new one will go there!"

"Where?"

"There...where I'm pointing... There!"

I have since found that pointing is pointless. One of the symptoms of Mike's Alzheimer's is the loss of direction, shape and space. Obviously, at the time, I didn't know this, and I got cross with him for being so difficult. As he was a marine engineer and had always done all home and garden tasks blindfolded, I assumed he was being awkward, resenting my involvement. I know better now.

I stormed off to the garden centre, shouting at him that I was going to buy the bloody panel.

By chance, at the top of the road, I met a friend, John. He was on his way back from the garden centre. He asked how I was, and I said that I was upset because of Mike's behaviour and told him what had happened. Instead of sympathising with me, as I had expected, he said: "Oh," with a shake of the head, "you shouldn't get angry with him."

I baulked.

I was totally taken aback; I couldn't understand why he was saying this. There wasn't anything wrong with Mike: he was just being deliberately awkward... wasn't he?

You make allowances for dotty, old people, not belligerent Mancunians. I was irritated with John for missing the point and for implying that there was something wrong with Mike.

It was the first time I'd considered that there could be anything amiss.

Shortly afterwards, we went to see the doctor about Mike's memory, and that was the beginning of a new chapter in our lives.

That was nearly five years ago. Mike has since gone through a metamorphosis on an alarming scale; the Alzheimer's, once named, started, imperceptibly at first, to erode my husband.

You can't look forward with dementia, only back. It's only when looking back that you see the changes that have happened.

But we mustn't give in to the future-stealing fiend and we must keep laughing.

Writing my blog became more difficult as the funny anecdotes began to dry up, but I discovered a new use for the posts: writing about the upsets was cathartic and helped me to calm down and to make sense of what was happening to us.

This next entry never actually made it onto my blog at the time as I felt it was too harrowing to share, but I am adding it here to my book, warts and all.

Deep, Dark Place

1st July 2017

I'm in a deep, dark place at the moment. I haven't posted for a long time because there hasn't really been much to laugh about, but I guess this is where the blog has to become more sombre.

I'm sitting over at the field, listening to the goats shouting for their dinner, the Shetland scratching her head on the wall of the stables and the chickens sorting out the pecking order (two are new).

This is my happy place: my sanctuary. So why are my eyes red raw and my throat swollen from crying?

Because I'm not coping.

Years from now, when Mike is gone, I will dwell on how I told him that I can't look after him anymore, and I will add it to the list of everything else in my life that I feel guilty about; it's a long list.

I've reached the point where it's no good people coming around after a crisis telling me how well I cope and that I have "a lot on my plate". I know I do; and I also know there are others far worse off than me.

I love my field. I'm not some rich landowner: I rent 3-and-a-quarter acres next to my house, and it's my hobby to look after the animals we've acquired. In 1994, I gave up smoking and Mike gave up 2 years later. I always vowed that I would use the money for something fun. At first, I used it for a gym membership, but for the past 10 years I have rented the field. (I found out how expensive cigarettes are the other day, and I was flabbergasted. A smoking habit nowadays costs far more than the rental on this little plot of land!)

Anyway, I feel like I'm trying to justify myself, but I also think I'm trying to work out how I can get so upset in a place I love.

Mike used to do everything over here, especially when he first retired. He would sort out the horses, the electric fencing, collection of thistles and brambles to feed the voracious goats, everything. Since he has had Alzheimer's, he has understandably done less and less, but he has still been able to obsessively collect weeds to feed the goats, which is a phenomenal help.

The upset today arose around Mike's inability to understand direct instructions. He has taken to pulling up weeds and putting a handful each in various buckets and barrows, or lids, or even just piles on the ground. This is fine, usually, and I just gather everything up together when it comes to feeding the goats. However, today, Mike threw a handful of nettles on the ground, near the barrow. Because I was there, and I wasn't wearing gloves, I asked him to pick them up and put them in the wheelbarrow, accompanying my request with pointing. Now, I know I mentioned that pointing was pointless in an earlier post, but I was so close that I was almost touching the nettles.

He just couldn't understand.

Mike kept pulling up more nettles and putting them on the original ones. I couldn't touch them, so I kept showing him and, eventually, I lost my temper.

Now before anyone berates me for being unreasonable, there's no need. I KNOW. I can usually keep my patience and understand that he can't help it. However, I'm off work with stress currently and my own mental health is poor.

So, realising that I had lost it, I apologised and went to sit down in a deckchair, asking Mike to join me. This was a further confusion for him, and he just couldn't understand what I wanted of him. At this point I dissolved into tears and rang Fred to come and get his dad. Yes, I needed some time away from my Mike to get my head together, but mainly because I wanted to protect *him* from *me*!

Fred appeared a few minutes later, brandishing a bottle of Budweiser for me (bless him) and took his dad back to the house to watch Manchester United on the TV, leaving me to regain my composure.

Which brings me back to the point of this post. Having written this, I am now completely calm, no longer crying, and thinking about a second Bud. When I get home, Mike will be pleased to see me and will give me a hug and a kiss as he always does. He won't clearly remember the upset, if at all, and he will probably tell me that my eyes look sore.

I now just need to come up with a new coping strategy for when this happens again, as no doubt it will.

_____

_____

Reflections – 2022

I mentioned a book earlier that was upsetting me but, once I got into it, I thoroughly enjoyed it. I wrote an online review.

Elizabeth Is Missing

23rd August 2017

I recently read Elizabeth is Missing by Emma Healey as it was recommended by a friend. I wouldn't normally have chosen a book with an Alzheimer's sufferer as the protagonist, and had I not paid for it as an audio book I wouldn't have continued past the first couple of chapters. It started off as a heart-breaking account of the day-to-day life of an elderly lady, Maud, treated like a child by her daughter and as an insignificance by her "carer". However, having paid for it, I persevered and was rewarded for doing so.

Cleverly, there is a plot based around an unsolved mystery from Maud's past. The memories from her youth are lucid and the writing reflects this, weaving us in to a compelling "whodunnit".

Meanwhile, the day-to-day life of Maud gives an insight into how a dementia sufferer may feel, taking us through the progression of the illness and the deterioration of the character from the perspective of the sufferer. There were bittersweet moments and times when I laughed aloud; the past tense mystery was quite a page-turner.

Personally, there were many times when I was listening to the book on my way to work when I wanted to turn the car around and go home to be understanding and patient with Mike. Many of Maud's thoughts explained a particular behaviour of Mike's and made them easier to deal with.

Whilst the subject was pertinent to me at that time in my life, I feel I should have read it earlier. I would recommend it as an essential read for anyone starting out on the journey of Alzheimer's, and an enjoyable, but instructive read for anyone else.

When we are in the car, Mike reads aloud road signs, adverts and placards as we pass them, and this is one of the behaviours included in the book. The constant reading out of visual words really annoys Maud's daughter in the novel, but it has yet to irritate me; I think it's one of the behaviours that I am more tolerant of, having sympathised with the character and having been forewarned.

The lack of understanding and aggression of some of the characters in the book made me protective of Maud, and, in turn, of Mike, and made me more aware of others who may be suffering from dementia. I have been thinking back to times in the past when I have thought that someone was either stupid or just weird, and I now realise, with shame, that they just needed a kind word or two rather than derisory comments and suppressed smirks.

Of course, there are still those who think that their knowledge of dementia that stems from a distant family member rather than someone they care for 24/7 needs to be shared with you. I was told last week that, "My sister-in-law just lays in bed staring at the ceiling. She doesn't know who anyone is." Yes, thanks for that. I really need the 'bleeding obvious' pointed out to me in a Basil Fawlty sort of way. It really helps me when I'm trying to make the best of the time Mike and I have left. Just a little understanding of how dementia affects those around them may help avoid thoughtless comments like that; Emma Healey's book could help to provide that understanding.

Reading Elizabeth is Missing really helped me to acknowledge a condition that I had no prior knowledge of, in an entertaining way. One of the characters in the TV comedy Benidorm was, in fact, reading it this week at the poolside: what more endorsement is needed?

My time as Mike's fulltime carer was coming to an end. I hadn't managed to get an au pair, despite lots of correspondence, and now Mike needed more than just company to get him through the day. Vicky had moved to our village to provide support and Mike would often wander up the road to her house or further on to the pub looking for me.

Social Services Care Package
20th September 2017

I've not posted much for a while because there is now less and less to laugh about. I have just had 3 months off work (yay!) because I had a breakdown (boo!) and I am on a phased return, only teaching. The coordination side of my job became impossible, largely because of one, particular colleague, but there had been a build-up of stress for months.

During my time off, Social Services have been brilliant. Our social worker, Cassie, has been a tower of strength for me in my fragile state, and has put together a care package for Mike that includes day care and personal assistants. Once I am back at work full time, I will have peace of mind, knowing that Mike is being looked after. It has been a tricky one to organise for Cassie, given the peripatetic nature and unsociable hours of my job. Mike has 3 different day care venues depending on where I am working, and 3 different personal assistants who come to the house to look after him.

It has been like having a toddler start playschool again. The first few times I dropped him off, I spent the time watching the clock, noting times when I knew he would be having lunch, or starting to look out for me.

There is no rhyme nor reason as to his reaction when I collect him: sometimes he reacts as if he hasn't seen me for ages, other times he acts like I've just been to the kitchen and back. However, he is always pleased to see me, and I am so grateful for that.

It's the same when I get back home after I have been teaching in the evenings, although the personal assistants are as equally pleased to see me as Mike is!

We settled into a routine for a while where I dropped Mike off at Wigston on a Tuesday, Earl Shilton on a Thursday, and Barwell on a Friday, and I worked in nearby adult learning centres. On Mondays and Wednesdays, when I had classes in the evenings, a carer would come to the house. All the carers were brilliant and provided Mike with stimulation, sustenance and safety.

The venue on a Friday was at the home of a couple, much older than Mike, who welcomed four or five clients daily, giving them the normality of a cosy, domestic setting rather than an institution, a wholesome, home-cooked lunch, and a chance to reminisce about their shared olden days. Although the venue was their own bungalow, they worked for Age UK. Everyone was treated as an individual: Mike used to take his BBC Wildlife magazines with him to show everyone, or one of the many photo books that I had printed for him, while one lady would sort a mountain of socks into pairs. I don't think she realised that they were the same socks each week, having been separated anew ready for her arrival.

I loved picking Mike up on a Friday as he was so "at home" and behaving relatively normally. I often stayed

for a cup of tea if there were still others to be collected,
although I was aware that this charming couple would
soon be off for a nap once the door had shut after their
last charge had left.

Pulling My Socks Up
11ᵗʰ November 2017

I met a lady today who made me realise that I need to
stop moping and start writing my blog again. In
September, I managed to delete my "notes" app from
my new phone and, when I reinstalled it, of course, all
my notes were gone. Among phone numbers and lists
were at least three almost finished posts and, more
alarmingly, several chapters of my book that don't exist
anywhere else. Fed up, I've not written anything since.

However, as I relaxed at the hairdressers' salon, having
my five-weekly counselling session, I was aware that the
lady in the next chair was quietly chuckling when I
brought humour into my outpouring of my life-
summary. It does me good to talk to Michelle about
Mike's decline amid our frantic life and she's a good
listener.

A little while later, the lady in the next chair leant over
and said: "I hope you don't think I've been listening on
purpose," (how could she not? I don't exactly babble in
hushed whispers) "but you've done me the power of
good."

I found out that this lady, Val, also had a husband with dementia. He was diagnosed two years ago so he is still at the stage where he can drive, follow written instructions and be left on his own. It made me quite nostalgic for those early days.

I haven't written a lot recently, as I said before, but that was partly because I had that repeated feeling that nothing was worthy of "laughing through" anymore. However, when I told Val how much improvement we had had by including super foods in our diet, albeit only for a year, I got back the urge to tell our story in case our experiences could help someone else. Val was saying that she regretted not having gone to Canada with her husband as now it was too late. I pointed out that, if they tried the super foods, they may not get such a profound improvement as we had, but it may just be enough to get them that trip to Canada.

Having chatted to Val today made me realise that there will always be someone out there whose Alzheimer's journey isn't as advanced as Mike's but who may be able to benefit from what we have found out further on up the road.

Reflections – 2022

To the non-scientific layperson, it seems to be a lottery as to who gets dementia and who doesn't. It certainly wasn't a prize we wanted but we didn't get a choice.

Four years after Mike's death from Alzheimer's, his brother, Ray, was diagnosed with vascular dementia, which must be extremely worrying for younger brother Bill, still only in his early sixties.

Most people know someone who has some form of dementia, but it's not always someone close enough to affect their own day to day lives. My next blog post deals with my early experience with dementia.

My Sainted Aunts

12ᵗʰ December 2017

Being the youngest child, of a youngest child, I grew up amid a different generation from my peers. My brothers were 8, 12 and 14 years older than me; my aunts and uncles were around the same age as my friends' grandparents: it's little wonder that I married a man old enough to be my father.

Consequently, I only had one grandparent, my lovely granny, Dad's mum. She died when I was 12 but I still keep things of hers to this day, much to the dismay of my super-tidy daughter-in-law.

Thinking about Granny, my ruminations today could start like the children's story, Snow White and Rose Red...

Once upon a time, there once was a lovely old lady who had two daughters. One daughter was gentle, kind and generous. She was a widow and she liked to bake cakes and to help people with their shopping and their housework. She was called Grace.

The other daughter was a bitter and twisted spinster who still lived with her mother and who loved to be mean to her sister whenever possible. She was called Gladys.

It's the stuff of fairy tales.

OK, back to normal narrative. As you may have worked out, I had a favourite: Aunty Grace. She was already 63 when I was born and I was often taken for her granddaughter during our holidays together, just the two of us, year after year in Guernsey, where she spoiled me rotten.

I was mystified as a child that neither of my aunties nor my granny could spell. In fact, Aunty Gladys even put an apostrophe in her own name, Glady's, much like the greengrocers and their infamous "tomatoe's" and "potatoe's". (Pause here while the punctuation pedants writhe on the floor, scratching the vision of rogue apostrophes from their eyeballs). I later realised that they had all had limited education, Granny having gone into service as a "tweenie maid" at the age of 13, and her daughters' schooling getting interrupted by a World War.

I also recognise, with hindsight and an adult mind, that Aunty Gladys probably had "issues" that a bit of CBT might have helped, but this was the '70s, so the child in me just saw a malevolent, cantankerous, old witch, who was deliberately evil to beloved Aunty Grace.

Anyway, I have become like Ronnie Corbett, and I have digressed.

As the aunts aged and needed more support, it was only natural that I should pay more attention to Aunty Grace, while the care of Aunty Gladys went to my cousin, Jean. She is my first cousin (sort of - you'll have to wait for the book for a full explanation as she's also my half niece, but don't hold your breath: I've been writing it since 1998) although she's two decades older than me. See what I mean? I'm just the baby in this family.

To get to the point, Aunty Grace was born with terrible eyesight and, in her latter years, was almost blind. However, she managed well and lived a full and active life until she was 88 and died in hospital after a fall that broke her hip.

Aunty Gladys, on the other hand, was mad!

Well, that's how I unkindly looked upon it in those days. I had never known anyone "senile", to use another less-than-sensitive term that was usual back then.

My first experience of dementia is with Mike. After years of feeling cheated that my mum only lived until she was 69, (I was only 31) I'm now relieved that neither she nor my dad had to suffer what Mike is going through now.

But then, let's look at this another way.

Aunty Gladys went into a home after her bed was found to be riddled with cigarette burns. It was a wonder she hadn't set the bed alight. In the care home she was only allowed to smoke in the dining room under supervision. Fair enough.

However, one day when I went to visit her, I found that she no longer smoked! Mike and I were incredulous as she had been a chain-smoker for over 40 years! It turned out that the people who ran the home had told her she had given up - and she believed them. Her body must have been craving nicotine terribly! I'm not sure about the moral side of their actions and if they would get away with it today, but she no longer smoked. Forever after, as she sat in her armchair, she would run her hand down the leg of the chair, as if looking for something... Of course, none of us was going to let on that she used to hang her handbag on the chair and that's where she kept her cigarettes.

So, there was Aunty Gladys, with some form of dementia, in a home, deprived of her human rights. Was she happy?

As a sand boy.

I would walk in and call out, "Hello, Aunty Gladys," and she would cheer and wave and come to greet me. She didn't remember me from Adam: if she had, she wouldn't have been so pleased to see me. During one of her lucid arguments with me when I challenged her treatment of Aunty Grace many years before, she had said, "I won't be dictated to by a 14-year-old." She wouldn't have greeted me as a long-lost friend if she had remembered that she didn't really like me.

On the other hand, Aunty Grace, fully compos mentis, could sometimes become very upset at her lack of vision and how she had to rely on others to do the simplest of tasks. She would say, quite simply, "I wish I could see." It was heart-breaking.

So, take from this what you will. Ultimately, will Mike be happier when the rest of his mind eventually goes? Will he be able to "enjoy" living again once he has forgotten who he used to be and what he used to like? Or would he have been better off with a physical disability, confined to a wheelchair or deprived of his sight, yet able to think for himself?

Life's a funny old game, isn't it?

Life continued and we survived another Christmas, but celebrations such as these only heightened Mike's decline as we all privately compared the current Mike/Dad/Grandad to the one from the year before.

Holiday?

22nd January 2018

I was considered brave by some for attempting a week away at New Year with Mike at this stage of his condition, especially since he had had a sharp decline for a few weeks in November. I did try to talk family members into going instead of us. It wasn't until Mike was put on to some new anti-psychotic medication that improved his mood that I was able to reconsider the trip.

As it turned out, we had a lovely time. There were just 3 times when I felt helpless and trapped, once ending up in the walk-in wardrobe to have a private conversation with my daughter-in-law, Leah, who kindly answered my plea for someone to talk to.

But there were moments of pure happiness when I was able to enjoy Mike's company completely. I think that I enjoyed myself even more because now, there is always that horrible realisation that there is no longer a guarantee, or sometimes even a likelihood, that we are going to be able to get through the ensuing hour without some form of upset.

On the evening of our first full day, we spent about an hour-and-a-half curled up on the sofa in the hotel bar, having a drink, a chat, and reading the newspapers. I went to the bar for a refill at one point and turned to check on Mike. He was sitting quietly, completely relaxed, looking through the newspaper. There was such an air of normality about him that nobody seeing him for the first time would have guessed that he had Alzheimer's. I was so proud of him.

The following evening, he wouldn't settle so we went up to the room instead, but I still feel grateful that we had that first evening.

There were other moments of pure happiness. Going to The Eden Project was very successful, two days on the trot. We were able to wander around the biomes, hand in hand, enjoying the stunning flora and each other's company, laughing often. Being on holiday and having no jobs to do, pets to look after or essays to mark made life so much easier. Mike thrives when he's getting attention and I was able to give him plenty.

I feel we made lots of nice memories during our week away which I documented with photos so I will always be able to reminisce. Mike made me laugh and made me proud, and I often felt that overwhelming surge of unconditional love that is more usually felt for a child. Mostly, though, it was that feeling of companionship that we've built up over the last thirty-odd years that I remember the most.

I've now booked our next holiday to Spain at Easter, and I really hope it will be as successful as Cornwall was so that I can spend quality time with Mike while it's still possible.

We continued to travel to lots of places; like a baby who sleeps well in a moving car, Mike was calm and content when being driven around, which is why I didn't baulk at driving all the way to Amiens in northern France, although the reason for going was not a good one.

Bittersweet

14th February 2018

It's funny how very good times can result from sad occurrences.

Our close French friend, Jacques, who lived in Amiens, died last month at the age of 82. He'd had "a good innings" as we Brits say, but it's still upsetting. I lived with Jacques and Christiane and went to a French school when I was a teenager. They had met my parents and become firm friends before I was even born. The tale has been told over and over, in English and in French.

As the story goes, my dad was driving through France in a lorry for work in 1960. My mum and my three brothers had accompanied him for some reason - I didn't think to ask how come while my parents were alive.

Anyway, the lorry broke down, apparently on a hill, in Abbeville in northern France, and Dad reversed it back down the hill to a Texaco station they had just passed.

Enter Christiane and Jacques, garage owners, and their toddler, Jacki.

To all intents and purposes, they made my future family very welcome for eight days while waiting for a lorry part to be delivered. Jacques and Dad had diagnosed the lorry problems with technical common words and lots of pointing, while Christiane manned the petrol pumps and my mum (who did speak French) looked after "little" Jacki. (Jacki grew up to become an American football player for Amiens so he didn't stay little for long)

For 8 days, Christiane, Jacques, Jacki, Christiane's brother, Regis, and my brothers all topped and tailed with very little bed space, while my parents slept over the road at an elderly neighbour's house.

My dad and Jacques talked motorbikes most of the time as Dad had been a scrambler and Jacques had a Triumph that needed work. A couple of weeks after this fateful meeting, Jacques was astonished when my dad's boss, Jack Stocker, a well-known rider with seven consecutive gold medals and who later became technical team manager to the International Six Days Trial (ISTD), turned up at the garage with the elusive part for his Triumph motorbike.

It was the start of a lifelong friendship, and when I say life long, in my case, it really was: Mum and Dad went to see them when they moved to Amiens in 1964, just before my October birth so there has never been a time for me when I didn't know them. My mum was a prolific letter writer and kept in touch, even when we emigrated to Canada in '66. We only lived there for a year and, once back in England, we visited Amiens at least once a year. The Chatelins also came to stay with us, as did various other family members on Christiane's side (she was the oldest of 7) who came for studies or holidays; they came with us on a massive family holiday in Aberystwyth when I was 11 and, as I said, I lived as part of their family when I went to school in Amiens, celebrating my 18th birthday with them during that time.

So, when I heard of Jacques' death, my first reaction to the news was to find someone to mind Mike so that I could be there for the funeral, but nobody was available, so I organised the next best thing: I took Mike with me but arrived the day after. I didn't think it was appropriate to take Mike to the service in case he said or did something to take the attention away from Jacques, and I thought the wake would be too stressful for him.

I'll never know if missing the funeral was a good call, but I'm certainly glad we went. Mike was "on form" from the moment we left home until the Eurotunnel on the way home, with a small lapse in the hotel bar in Calais when he panicked and needed to go back to the room.

Seeing Christiane did the pair of us the power of good, and I hope we helped her too. Since my mum died in

1996, I've called Christiane my "other mother" and I never go to France without seeing her. Mike is also very fond of Christiane, and he was totally at ease sitting at her table, drinking wine, eating whatever was put in front of him and giving the occasional, "ça va," when prompted. I was really enjoying spending time with Christiane, two of her sisters and her 27-year-old grandson, but I was expecting at any minute that it would be all over and that I would have to take Mike for a walk to change the scenery as he becomes fretful when his attention span is reached.

But it never happened.

It was a lovely, restful, therapeutic time for both of us. On top of that, I was able to support Christiane and I have another good memory to add to my collection.

It was never possible to document everything that happened to us, and I wasn't keen to write about the many upsets we had. I was just grateful for the times when everything was going well.

Ups and Downs
19th February 2018

We've had a few relatively good weeks since we got back from our New Year in Cornwall. Instead of several hours of upset every day, we were having a couple of bad hours every other day. I was beginning to think I could take on the world again. In fact, somebody at work actually accused me of being cheerful!

However, I knew it wouldn't last, and we had three bad days on the trot, which left me feeling like I needed to escape again, albeit temporarily.

Things then came to a head one evening before half term, while I was trying to cook, unpack the shopping and convince Mike that we were indeed in our own house. I knew I was getting stressed so started to ring round the family for someone to chat to who didn't have Alzheimer's. It soon became apparent that nobody was picking up the phone. I put a message on our family WhatsApp group, to no avail. I then remembered a little bird telling me that someone in the family had advised not answering the phone to me when I was upset, presumably to stop me from becoming dependent on them. I've no idea who suggested this. This upsets me because they have no idea how much I cope with before I crack, and this was the first time I'd cried since Cornwall.

Anyway, in a fit of pique, I petulantly committed the social media equivalent of throwing myself under a bus: I left the group! "That'll teach them," I thought. "They'll be sorry." Of course, it doesn't have quite the same impact as the actual bus thing but I was making a point, which was picked up by James who, in an act of solidarity, joined me back in the group again. Good boy.

I'm due to go away for my annual girlie weekend in London at the end of this week. It's amazing the difference 12 months has made as, this time last year, I was able to leave Mike at home with Fred and Renée. This year the plan was for Vicky to come and stop here for the weekend to look after her dad and the animals. However, Mike's deterioration has meant that Vicky was very worried about doing this and we looked at respite care, which was singularly unsuccessful. Suffice it to say that Mike was "too young" for the care home we tried out. He only went for a few hours, but he burst into tears when I picked him up. He was sitting at the end of a row of high-backed chairs which were occupied by old folk in various stages of recumbent posture, some overhanging the chair completely, some slightly slouched and others relatively upright but asleep. Mike's not ready for that yet. We have since found a more suitable place, but not in time for my London trip.

Luckily, I have a brother who was a complete tyrant when I was young, but who has now turned into a jolly nice chap, thanks largely to his wife. Thankfully, they will come down from Yorkshire to support Vicky for the weekend while I'm away. They did this 3 years ago when Fred was in hospital, which was a lifesaver. Clive's only proviso this time is that he's not spending the weekend picking up bloody dog muck!

So, things are up and down but we keep plodding on. The ups far outweigh the downs, although I'm not sure one of our carers, Doris, would agree after binning her slippers yesterday, having had to chase Mike over the field when he decided suddenly to leave the garden, climb over the electric fence and wade through the mud to join me at the stables, but we have fun times too.

We obviously appear to be coping too well at the moment, so Lady Luck sent us a new game: Mike had his first appointment at the oncology out-patients last week, but that's another story.

I did indeed go away for my girlie weekend. It was actually paid for by Social Services, theatre tickets and all. I was able to claim it as a carer for respite and it was all totally legal. However, when I tried to claim for blackout curtains for the bedroom so that Mike didn't keep getting up at the crack of dawn, I was told that it wasn't a claimable item...

Anyway, I relaxed totally while away and had a great time. My next post includes Facebook communication after the trip from all those who put themselves out so that I could unwind.

In Others' Shoes
3rd March 2018

Last weekend in London with Toni was great fun. I certainly needed the break, and I was happy knowing that Mike was being well cared for.

However, my poor stepdaughter, Vicky, and my brother and his wife, Clive and Pam, were finding caring for Mike a lot more difficult than I had expected them to. Thankfully, they were all kind enough not to tell me this while I was away.

I thanked them all and brought little gifts back, and then, since we live in the digital age, I thanked them via Facebook. Their replies were frank, funny and philosophical.

My post:

I had a great weekend in London with Toni thanks to Clive, Pam and Victoria who wore themselves out looking after Mike for me. You're all stars ✸ ✿ ✫

Pam replied:

You are more than welcome, and it was nothing that couldn't be sorted by a good night's sleep! X

Clive wrote at length:

I felt better as soon as I got in the car! But that could have been down to the fact that I was holding a steering wheel and knew what I was supposed to do with it! A rare situation all weekend!

My main contribution was to keep out of the way whenever possible. I even volunteered to wash-up and cook fried eggs just to be in another room.

It was surreal. There is a lot going on in Mike's head but none of it connects properly if Cathryn isn't present. It's as though she is an important conduit in his brain.

To me, it appeared that Mike was stuck in one of those dreams where everything goes wrong or turns out to be different from how it started off. Very difficult to deal with but Vicky deserves a medal, as does Pam.

The love that Vicky has for her dad overcomes the fact that he doesn't know who she is best part of the time. Mike firmly believed that Vicky was our daughter. Before I realised what the situation was, Mike and I were looking out of the patio doors when Vicky was in the field. Vicky had just gone out of sight, and he said, "Where's your daughter gone to?" When I said that Vicky was his daughter, he reacted as though I was suggesting that something inappropriate had gone on between him and Pam!

Pam responded:

Cathryn certainly deserves a medal for her 24/7 love & devotion to Mike. To see his face light up, on her return, was truly a joy to behold!

Clive added, hilariously:

Only matched by the look of shear relief on the faces of the other three people in the room!

Having read all these comments, Toni interjected:

Thought you would like to know all your efforts were very much appreciated. Cathryn had a lovely weekend, and it was good to see her relaxing, if only for a few days, so I thank you all as well.

Pam answered:

Thanks Toni. It was knowing that Cathryn could relax & enjoy herself that spurred us all on! Good to know that you (also) had a great time.

Then my youngest brother commented. Simon used to race Formula Ford 2000 and Mike was his mechanic. Simon had great faith in Mike's ability and often, much like the Elves and the Shoemaker, where leather was left out overnight and the following morning brand new shoes would be made, Simon used to leave gears in his garage for Mike to change ready for an upcoming race. Mike would often turn up after Simon went to bed or before he got up in the morning and so became known as "The Gearbox Fairy".

Simon said:

Wow, this made me fill up. A devastating illness for all concerned. Not seeing Mike on a regular basis he's still the gearbox fairy in my head. It's heart breaking to read what his illness has done to him and Cathryn.

Clive succinctly finished with:

I think that Vicky summed it up nicely when we took Mike to Bradgate Park: "Alzhiemer's is shit!"

Reflections - 2022

After having had a very bad experience the first time I tried to leave Mike in a care home, albeit only for a day, I wasn't keen to try it again. However, I was convinced by those who knew better than me that the first care home, full of elderly dementia sufferers in the late stages of their conditions, was not typical of all care homes and that I would be able to find one more suitable to meet Mike's needs and not leave him traumatised as the first one had.

Grieving for the Living
9ᵗʰ March 2018

I don't know how many times I'm going to have to grieve for Mike while he's still alive, but today was another step towards finality, and I feel like my heart is being wrenched out through my throat.

I've just spent three-and-a-half hours "dropping" Mike at a local care home, having put off the morning appointment as I wanted to spend more time with him. We visited the home for the first time on Wednesday evening, after staff from the home had come out to assess him that morning. Everything has moved so quickly since then that I can't quite believe it has happened and he's actually there.

I've left him!

Respite has been on the cards for some time now, and the need for respite care, rather than relying on family, was reinforced when I recently went to London for the weekend and left Mike in the care of his daughter, my eldest brother and my sister-in-law. You may have read my post about how they coped but, if not, I can tell you that they didn't find it a picnic.

However, leaving Mike with three family members for the weekend gave me exhilarating feelings of freedom, escape and liberty; abandoning him at the care home this evening has left me bereft.

I got upset over something stupid at work on Thursday and realised that I was probably feeling emotional because of the impending respite, so I knew that I wasn't going to find the experience, when it came to it, a walk in the park.

Indeed, my appointment to drop Mike off was at 10:30 this morning but I put it off until 11.30, then lunchtime, then after lunch, then 2:30pm. I felt like I was tricking Mike when I finally asked him to get in the car to make the journey (well I was).

As we arrived, Mike started to smell a rat, but I was able to convince him that he should get out of the car and enter the building. Once inside, the presence of a cycloptic cat took Mike's attention and he immediately relaxed, taking the introductions in his stride and even showing an interest in the room he'd been allocated which, coincidentally, had his name on the door.

There was a ton of paperwork to get through to take my mind off the inevitable time that I would have to leave but, once that was completed, and Mike's meagre possessions were unpacked, reality took over again and I found myself biting back tears. If only he could have been behaving unreasonably today, I was thinking, then I would have been keen to get out. But he wasn't. He had been lovely all day, and all day I had been wanting to cancel the whole thing. "How did it come to this?" Mike asked out of the blue, and we both clung to each other and cried.

We went for a wander round the corridors and were then ushered down to the dining room for "tea" (novel - we're lunch and dinner people). The staff had organised for us to sit with a resident called Clive, who was a nonagenarian, retired steam engineer, most interested in the fact that Mike was a retired marine engineer. Despite the clanking of plates and singalong music, Mike and Clive were able to discuss the Clifton Suspension Bridge, Isambard Kingdom Brunel and the SS Great Britain.

I kept thinking that I should say goodbye and leave, but I couldn't bring myself to. Every time I thought about it, I started to choke up and then Mike would get tears in his eyes too.

Then, suddenly, Mike said: "Will you get home alright?"

"Yes, I'll be fine," I assured him, with the realisation that he knew I was leaving him there, which obviously got my eyes leaking again.

Our dining companion asked Mike, "What's the problem, then?"

I told him, "Alzheimer's."

"That's very sad," he said, and I agree, it's bloody sad that we are having to go through this. Mike doesn't look his 72 years, and he certainly doesn't look like there is anything wrong with him at first glances. It's heart-breaking that he still looks like the man I married and still sometimes behaves like him, but this human, who has contributed to society, who has fathered 5 children, who has loved and been loved, can no longer participate in real life and must just be tolerated, humoured and excused until the Grim Reaper chooses to take away the physical form that will be left behind once this bastard disease has taken everything else from my lovely husband.

I came home to my empty house full of dogs, to cry. I hope I've pulled myself together by Sunday, the day after tomorrow, when I can fetch Mike. This is supposed to be for my benefit but all it feels like is another virtual bereavement in a long line of virtual bereavements that I've had to experience since Mike's diagnosis 6 years ago.

Reflections – 2022

The respite did actually go well, and I was desperate to see Mike when I picked him up. I realised that everyone telling me to have some time to myself to recharge my batteries had been right and that it was going to have to become the new normality.

Forgive me readers: it's been two weeks since my last post!

24th March 2018

I should have posted to say how successful the respite was; that Mike had been fine; that it was lovely to see him again because I had missed him so much; that I had become more patient and tolerant with him as a result of the short absence; that I would recommend respite to anyone in my position; that I haven't cried since leaving him there.

But I didn't write it soon enough.

This evening, we have taken a backward step and I'm feeling utterly exhausted by Mike's behaviour since we finished dinner. I'm not sure if he's gone downhill, or if my tolerance levels have dipped.

I know I was tetchy at work yesterday but that may have been because I was rushing to get jobs done before going on annual leave for Easter. Maybe I'm subconsciously worried about two weeks of being Mike's 24/7 carer, with no day-care and no visiting carers until I'm back at work. Whatever the reason, this evening has been dire and has brought me to tears again for the first time since leaving Mike in the home.

When enquiring about Mike's health, many people ask me, sympathetically, "Has his memory got worse then?" These are the people who have been fortunate enough not to have anyone with Alzheimer's in the family; or who have been visitors of dementia sufferers when they are being cared for by someone else. These are the well-meaning people who think that having Alzheimer's equates to memory loss only.

I was guilty of it myself. I was quite ambivalent about my aunt having dementia when I visited annually, as it didn't affect my life at all.

Memory loss is the least of Mike's problems.

It's eating sausage, mash and peas with a knife, just a knife; it's getting undressed immediately after getting dressed, despite being told not to by the person desperately trying to get themselves ready for work; it's being unable to go through a door because the process of turning the handle while working out whether to pull or push is too difficult; it's standing up but believing themselves to be sitting down, so not understanding the repeated request to "sit down"; it's handing someone an envelope when they've been asked to pass the telephone; it's obsessive toilet roll folding; it's losing the settee; it's seeing things that aren't there, and not seeing things that are there; it's the loss of all concept of time; it's having no spatial awareness; it's vile.

I have been writing this in bed on my iPhone, waiting for tonight's obsessive behaviour to end. Judging by his breathing, Mike has finally dropped off so it's probably safe for me to get some sleep. I'll get a couple of hours before the toilet trips start again. This will have nothing to do with his Alzheimer's, and everything to do with his prostate cancer, but that would require a whole new blog.

Goodnight.

Reflections – 2022

I had been looking forward to Easter in Spain since my trip to Cornwall at New Year, but the incremental changes in Mike meant that I knew I could no longer do it alone. Luckily, Mike's brother, Bill, was available and agreed to holiday with us.

Planes, Buggies and Automobiles
3rd April 2018

There's nothing like sitting on your balcony, drinking tea, listening to the birds sing, and looking out over the Mediterranean Sea to provide an antidote to a terrible night's sleep.

However, that relaxed feeling disappears instantly when you realise that your husband is no longer in the building, as you had thought, and has gone walkabout!

We have him back now, but it has just about killed Bill, with his newly diagnosed asthma, as he ran up and down the wrong hill on a well-meaning wild goose chase. I threw on a pair of jeans and tucked my nightie into the waistband before running out into the Spanish sunshine after him. I ran directly to reception for assistance with the search, with a view to pushing in in front of everyone being served at the desk, only to find that one of the people was in fact Mike, who was with a lovely lady and two children. It was her husband who had sent Bill in the wrong direction, but it was also her husband who had chased after Bill once they had found the missing pensioner.

Mike didn't seem at all disturbed by the experience and came back to the apartment holding my hand, chatting happily and wondering why Bill and I were worried!

We have been in Spain since Thursday, but Mike and I spent the first couple of days 3 hours up the coast at my brother's in Almeria, where we had a lovely time reminiscing, drinking, eating tapas and playing darts with Simon and Mary. It was a really nice interlude and Mike was on form which was brilliant. There was a poignant moment when we left, however, when Simon put his brother-in-law's seatbelt on for him. For years, it was Mike who strapped Simon into his FF2000 single seater racing car and this irony was felt by all, except Mike

Our journey had begun quite promisingly. Vicky dropped us at the airport and we went straight to the

Jet2 assistance desk. It was unmanned so I found myself speaking to a tiny man in box below the counter who urged me to sit Mike in a wheelchair and to hurry to Gate 10 as boarding was commencing in 5 minutes! Luckily, Mike didn't make a fuss about being in a wheelchair but hurrying proved more difficult than expected since the only way the chair would move forward was if the handle was squeezed whilst pushing. I found that rather difficult with my arthritic thumbs, and the only way I managed, whilst simultaneously pulling a case on wheels, was to constantly crash into things and apologise profusely to Mike. I thought the other passengers would be waiting irritably for us but, when we arrived at Gate 10, a man in a high vis jacket at the head of the queue greeted us with: "Blimey; you didn't hang about!" and proceeded get us boarded and settled and I didn't have to lift another finger, arthritic or not.

It was much the same when we landed in Malaga, but this time staff took us on a buggy along underground corridors at what felt like such high speed that it reminded me of being on an airboat on the Everglades. It was fantastic and had Mike shouting: "Whee!"

Once transferred to the car hire place, I was coerced into taking out extortionately priced insurance by a snotty Spanish youth. However, he then upgraded us to a brand-new BMX M series from a Corsa for some unknown reason. I was asked via Facebook by my stepson if I knew how to drive a decent car. Cheek! I wasn't even aware that it was considered "decent", but I was subsequently told that it was a sporty model so, on the way back to Malaga from my brother's, I experimented, and I found out it had quite a lot of grunt, enjoying the drive immensely, much more than when I first drove it.

At the beginning, I found the best way to get used to the gear stick being on my right was to get stuck in the town around Malaga Airport and continually make U turns, slamming the back of my left hand into the door every time I tried to change gear.

Unfortunately, Mike got very anxious at this point and, every time I did a U turn or pulled up for a 3-point turn, he tried to get out of the car. Thank goodness it took me 4 days to find out how to unlock the doors without the key or he would have been off!

Once I finally found the motorway, he also got angry every time I veered onto the rumble strip, which was often to start with, and he shouted at the bastards who were making the car vibrate. I kept trying to explain that it was me trying to get used to the width of the BMW that caused the noisy reverberations, but he continued to vent his anger towards the Spanish.

Anyway, Bill has been doing the driving since he got here on Saturday and he's much better at it than me, although I did brace myself somewhat today, seconds before we pulled onto the motorway from a stop sign (seriously), my bro-in-law announcing excitedly: "Thank goodness we've got the M Series!"

Reflections – 2022

In retrospect, I am clearly able to see that the holiday in Spain was the beginning of the end. In fact, I think we left something of the real Mike with Simon as I never properly saw that same person again.

It was while we were in our luxury apartment in Fuenguirola that Mike began the downward spiral of incontinence, and from then the deterioration came on in leaps and bounds. I found him one night, standing in the bath, hosing himself down with the hand-held shower attachment as he had had an accident. I led him to the shower cubicle and got him all fresh again but there then followed days of obsession with the toilet. We ordered dinner one evening in the restaurant and, while we waited, Mike visited the toilet four times, never being able to sit back down for longer than a couple of minutes. We changed the order to a takeout so that we could go back to the apartment to eat and so that Mike could visit the loo when he wanted to, without me having to go with him. This went on for a couple of days and we were pretty much confined to barracks, albeit rather luxurious barracks with a jacuzzi and all mod cons.

Then one morning, Mike looked up to the mountains from the balcony and announced: "That's where I want *to go." I immediately fetched Bill who got dressed and brought the car round. We went up into Mijas Pueblo where we spent a lovely afternoon and I made sure I took lots of photos to document such a good time. I'm glad I did as we didn't have much more time before Mike went into a home for good.*

Don't Forget To Leave The Toilet Seat Up! 21ˢᵗ April 2018

I have spent my life surrounded by men. I grew up with three older brothers, and I produced two sons: no female DNA in sight, apart from Mum and me (scientifically incorrect but that's the term I want to use).

I don't remember the toilet seat as being much of an issue when I was a child: it was always up so I put it down. I don't think we actually had a lid to the loo, but I was aware, as I grew up, that leaving it up was a source of stereotypical, nagging-woman humour.

Mike always put the lid and the seat back down; in fact, when he redesigned and rebuilt our downstairs bathroom, he made it so that you couldn't flush without putting the lid down. Clever!

Sadly now, one of my many coping tasks is to make sure the seats and lids are up, partly so that Mike recognises the toilet more clearly, and partly to ensure that there is as little as possible to clear up off the floor. During the night for the past 6 months, I have had to get up every time Mike does (on average four times due to his prostate cancer) just to check that he has found the correct receptacle, and that the seat is in the correct position for number ones or number twos. However, sometimes I sleep so heavily that I just have to face whatever he's managed, be it in the sink, the shower, a plastic tub or all over the closed lid, the latter obviously causing far more cleaning than the other choices.

I don't mind, but I have been advised that Mike should now be getting the higher rate of attendance allowance because of his night-time shenanigans. These are the things you find out by accident. Nobody comes to you and says, "Here: have more money!"

My dad lived with us for the last six months of his life following a heart attack. I was pregnant when he came, and there followed a race to give birth before Dad's heart gave up. I used to come downstairs in the morning and check that he was still breathing, before going to get breakfast. It took its toll on my health, but Dad lived long enough to meet his new grandson.

The first eleven weeks of Fred's life were the last eleven weeks of Dad's. I'm forever grateful that they were able to meet, the oldest and the youngest of this heavy family branch, but they made each other's existence more difficult, albeit for only a short while.

The nights were particularly difficult: the 4am feed would disturb Dad, and the midnight wandering would disturb Fred. I wanted to enjoy time with my precious new-born, yet I was trying to make the most of what I knew would be my final memories of my last remaining parent.

I found out afterwards that we would have been entitled to a night carer, someone whose job it would have been to stay awake and care for Dad, while I cared for my baby. I would have been less of a zombie during the daytime and more able to be a proper daughter.

In retrospect, I wish I had just spent money to ease the situation. I should have paid for more care for Dad so that Mike could have been with me at the hospital during Fred's first 6 days; I should have paid for someone to run my 13-year-old son to rehearsals and back so that Mike wasn't exhausted; I should have paid for night care so that we could all have been better rested. While I was in hospital, poor Mike would look after Dad and send Joe off to school, waiting for the carer; he would then go to work for his typical long hours, then race back to take Joe to the theatre, home again to wait for my brother to sit with Dad and then finally get to spend a few minutes with his new boy, before being turfed out of the hospital at the end of visiting. By the time he got there, he had missed so many "lovely moments" that he was faced with an accusing, maniacal wife who had been watching the door for the previous four hours for her husband to share precious expressions, sounds and windy smiles.

Over the past two years, as Mike has deteriorated and been unable to look after our menagerie, I have taken on yard hands. At first it was just a couple of times a week when I was working in the evening, to help Mike with the tasks, but as the disease progressed, so did my need for help at the field. The family was helpful to start with, but the need outgrew their capacity, so I took on more help. Now, I have a yard hand 6 days a week. My philosophy with a problem now is to throw money at it. This would be brilliant if I actually had any, but I figure I can work something out later. The important thing now is to enjoy my time with Mike where possible. I learned that from Dad.

So, because of this new philosophy, Mike is in the care home tonight and tomorrow night so that I can recharge my batteries and be a better carer when I collect him on Sunday. It's only his second stay there and I found it slightly easier to leave him this time: only an hour-and-a-half, and I cried less! I rang this evening to see how he was. He was "fine" but he had just got out of the fire escape! "We got him back in," I was reassured.

However, I mentioned recharging my batteries, and what am I doing? I'm writing my blog in the middle of the night... Doh!

So, with the toilet seats and lids firmly down, I bid you goodnight.

We were entering a whole new phase of decline, and Mike's deterioration was becoming more rapid. There was no longer any need to convince people we met that he had Alzheimer's: it was obvious.

Anniversary blues
27ᵗʰ May 2018

This time last year I referred to Mike, on my Facebook profile, as my soulmate, my playmate, and my best mate. This year, my mate has disappeared, replaced by a clingy, needy, child-like replica of the man I married 28 years ago today.

Mike's deterioration, following his diagnosis of Alzheimer's about 5 years ago, has been gradual, most of the outside world not even realising that he had it until last summer. Frighteningly, the last 6 months have seen the biggest changes. Whereas before he was tiptoeing tentatively into this new and strange world, he is now striding towards oblivion in seven-league-boots.

I've recently had a glimpse of the not-too-distant future and it's quite terrifying. Last week, Mike got a urinary tract infection. This can knock an able-bodied rugby player for six but, coupled with Alzheimer's, the UTI left him like a ragdoll: a heavy ragdoll; a ragdoll who wouldn't bend his legs; a ragdoll who needed to be carried lifted and bent just to get him to sit down. I wasn't able to manage him alone. Being 19 years younger than Mike, you would think would make me an ideal carer, but at 53 I already have arthritis in my hands and a fragile mental state: thank goodness for Vicky and thank goodness for antibiotics!

Mike was such an able, capable, and knowledgeable person. He could turn his hand to anything, having been a marine engineer, even sewing! When he retired, I was spoilt rotten, coming home from work to find a tidy house, the ironing done, the plumbing sorted and dinner on the table.

I have always counted myself lucky to be married to my best friend. Of course, we argued: we were living a real married life, not a fairy tale. My vicious and violent vitriol was matched against Mike's cool, supercilious, and patronising put-downs. But we were more than happy together for most of the time.

This 28th anniversary of our nuptials is the first as Mike's carer, rather than his wife. I knew it was going to happen sooner or later, but I do miss him.

We did have a lovely wedding and we always reminisce on this day, but today has been difficult, not just due to Mike's condition but also because of poignant news from overseas.

Our wedding was attended by a special guest of honour from Canada, who sang in the church while we signed the register: my Aunty June. She sang Morning has

Broken beautifully, despite the 84-year-old organist losing most of the correct notes!

Unfortunately, I found out this afternoon that she died last night following a long battle with dementia. It wasn't unexpected but it's still so sad, especially today as we had talked to Mike's carer about spending one night of our honeymoon with her, Uncle Peter and my two cousins, Jo and Sue. I had explained that, after my mum died, Aunty June became quite a comfort to me as she was so like her big sister, albeit much taller. Even though they were an ocean apart, Mum and Aunty June corresponded so regularly that it was much like the social media of today, which I'm sure they would have both embraced. I always felt very close to my aunt and was shocked to see her so diminished on the last occasion that we were together, a few years ago, during a stop-over in London. I had known she had dementia, but I hadn't been prepared to see my lovely aunt looking so tiny and lost in a Heathrow hotel bed. Mike and I had dinner with her and with Uncle Peter before they flew off to their holiday destination. I will always be glad that we made the journey to see them, even though it was only for a few hours, and I never imagined for a minute that, one day, when I was to hear of her passing, that my own Mike would be heading down the same route.

And so, it's with a heavy heart that I say: "Happy Anniversary to my darling Mike; and Rest In Peace Aunty June."

Reflections – 2022

At the beginning of the journey when Mike knew that he had an illness, we would have comical conversations that made us both laugh. On one occasion, he announced, "These bloody flies!"

"What flies?" I asked.

"The ones I can see and you can't," he replied.

However, as his Alzheimer's progressed and he was not aware of the fact that he was seeing things differently, I learned an important rule: it is imperative that you enter "their" world, as they can no longer access the real one. I have witnessed people arguing with dementia sufferers and it is completely pointless.

The next blog post explores this idea.

The Emperor's New Clothes
3rd June 2018

Nobody can say for sure how an Alzheimer's sufferer sees the world, but there's plenty of documentation to suggest that it's not how the rest of us see it.

In the early stages of Mike's illness, when he could still articulate his observations on his condition, the bedroom ceiling would go green. We would discuss the fact that I could see it was white and he knew he was seeing it differently, wondering what it was in his brain that made the colour appear so. It still goes green now, as do other things, but there is no longer a discussion about it; I just agree.

I'm agreeing with all sorts these days. I live in a land of perpetual make-believe, taking invisible objects from Mike and nodding at comments to do with things that just aren't there: animals, cars, food, etc. In fact, even though he gave up 20 years ago, I caught him smoking an invisible cigarette at the stable today! I'm not condoning that imaginary habit I can assure you.

However, the most unnerving of Mike's visions are when he refers to the other people in the room, and we're alone... I try not to let it freak me out, but it does get a bit creepy in the evening when he starts to whisper and it's just the two of us. If I ask him why he's whispering, he will shush me and surreptitiously incline his head towards the invisible intruders.

Of course, I'm mostly a sceptical and cynical person when it comes to things that can't be proven but, in the words of Hamlet: "There are more things in Heaven and Earth, Horatio, than are dreamt of in your philosophy," and there's certainly some weird stuff going on in my husband's brain.

Agreeing with Mike, whatever he says, seems to be the easiest way to keep things on an even keel. Christine, who runs the group at Age UK, advised me long ago not to argue with Mike and it does seem to keep him happy, but it's not always easy to humour him when I'm tired or stressed: the woman in me hates the man getting the last word!

Anyway, it's time to sleep now so let's hope the blokes in the corner of the room don't disturb us while they're painting over the green ceiling with a flamingo.

Reflections – 2022

Since the first awful experience with a care home, whenever I considered a home for Mike, we always went together to visit it, to find out if it was suitable. In fact, there was one just down the road from us, walking distance on a nice day, that seemed ideal. It gets a mention in a later blog post. It was full, but Mike was added to the waiting list. It was an unpleasant situation, waiting for someone to die, but that was the reality.

However, Mike never made it to that home because fate took control and shaped the rest of his life.

Without a visit to see what it was like, Mike went into a different home in Wigston on 10th June 2018, purely because it was the only one that could take him at short notice, and it was definitely an emergency.

Vicious Circles

12th June 2018

Mike's not just in a vicious circle: he's in a vicious, evil, and vindictive circle.

Currently I am with him in the Leicester Royal Infirmary, waiting for him to have his hip X-rayed.

Why does he need an X-ray? You ask.

Because he had a fall.

How did he fall?

I don't know; I wasn't there.

Why weren't you there?

Because he was in a care home for respite.

Why did you need respite?

Because I couldn't cope any more.

Why couldn't you cope?

Because he got into a psychotic loop and ended up with a UTI just days after finishing antibiotics for the previous UTI.

Why did he have a UTI?

Well, therein lies the crux of the matter...

A lot has happened since I last wrote an entry.

To explain, Mike gets into what has been described as psychotic loops, where an action causes another action which, in turn, causes the original action all over again; and so it continues. We get a lot of these at night which is why I get so little chance to sleep. Believe me, given the opportunity, I can sleep for England; I can even sleep on a cross-Channel ferry!

One such loop is getting out of bed to go to the toilet; finding the bed sheet rumpled and smoothing it; having just smoothed the sheet, he believes he was getting back into bed so he gets in rigidly with his knees and sometimes his feet sticking out of the side of the bed; I get up to lift his legs in; he goes back to sleep; he wakes because he never made it to the toilet so he needs a wee; he gets up and notices the sheet is rumpled; yada, yada, yada.

A few weeks ago, Mike started to find it difficult to sit on the toilet. Social Services had arranged for a grab rail near the downstairs toilet, but it didn't seem to help just on the one side. I ordered a commode which was equally unsuccessful. I ended up going purposely to places that had disabled facilities: our local garden centre, shopping centres, McDonald's!

In my unqualified opinion, being literally anally retentive is the reason he got his first urinary tract infection. Unfortunately, UTIs are notorious in the elderly for causing confusion. The combination of Alzheimer's and extra confusion equalled a nightmare scenario, and we're still in it.

My family had been urging me to let Mike have some time in respite to recharge my own batteries, but I was fighting them every inch of the way. This wasn't a parent whom I'd moved away from to start a new life once I'd grown up: this was my husband, with whom I'd chosen and vowed to spend the rest of my life.

But I had a terrible wake-up call in the early hours of the morning a couple of Sundays back, after days of finding it difficult to cope. I found myself trapped in an impossible situation in the bathroom with absolutely no ability to put it right. Mike's legs and feet and pyjama bottoms that were round his ankles, were covered with excrement, and so was the carpet, all the way back to the bed. I later found out it was the bed too. I asked Mike to lift his foot to get out of his pyjamas and into the shower so that I could clean him, but he didn't understand what I meant. The step into the shower is about 6 inches off the ground and he just could not lift his foot to get in, nor could he lift it high enough for me to remove the pyjamas. My phone was on the bed, but I couldn't go and get it as, every time I let go of Mike, he tried to walk out of the bathroom, so I was unable to call for help. I realised in that moment that I didn't have the facilities, the strength, or the mental stability to care for my husband's complex and urgent needs. As I burst into tears at the enormity of the realisation, the deeply buried "real" Mike bubbled to the surface to console me. I clung to those few moments of lucidity to sort out the immediate problem. In his need to care for me, he suddenly remembered how to lift his foot and he got into the shower. Since then, I have known that my days as his main carer are coming to an end. This chapter is nearly over.

So, back to today. Mike is going to be admitted to a ward whether his hip is broken or just bruised, and all I can do is be here for him as he drifts in and out of wakefulness.

Maybe if he hadn't been in that care home this morning he wouldn't have fallen; but maybe something worse could've happened to him in my "care".

Reflections – 2022

Mike's hip became a recurring theme that would become problematic right up until the end and would need yet another hospital visit, which would also be farcical, but not as bad as the one I wrote about in the next post.

The Empty Bed
20th June 2018

I have always loved the song The Empty Bed by Mick Ronson (Google it) but I never realised that the lyrics would become so poignant for me. Of course, I use the word "empty" metaphorically: with four dogs and two cats, my bed is rarely really empty. When Mike went into respite the first time, I made sure to take at least one dog to bed with me. It's nice to have something to cuddle, and whippets are mega cuddly. Ask anyone in the Whippet Appreciation Society.

  However, by Mike's third respite, I was enjoying the space to stretch out in bed, and the canines were relegated downstairs. It was lovely to have the whole bed to myself; I used to enjoy the same occasional treat in the past when Mike fell asleep downstairs, but it was occasional. Mainly, I enjoyed sharing my bed with my husband and cuddling up to him (especially when my feet were cold, which is almost always).

For the past two weeks, I have had the house, and the bed, to myself. Mike went into emergency respite when I got to breaking point. He was supposed to be coming home tomorrow but I have extended his stay; I don't yet know if he will stay there for another week, another month, or forever.

You may have read about Mike's fall last week in the home, when he was taken to hospital. What I haven't written about is the farce that ensued. To cut a long story short, the NHS actually lost him: he "wasn't at the hospital", and he wasn't back at the care home. I was obviously totally calm throughout this débâcle (not). I had been fully expecting to stay with him at the hospital overnight, but staff on the ward made it clear that I was to leave.

The next day, apparently, the ward discharged him and sent him to the ambulance waiting area to be returned to the home, without any mention of him having Alzheimer's! He waited there in a wheelchair for hours, with his legs covered by a blanket as he didn't have his trousers on. He could have wandered off at any time. When the drivers tried to take him to the ambulance, they reported that he seemed "confused" (Really?) and so they wouldn't take him. I still feel guilty that I left him there on his own. I should have insisted on staying.

Anyway, the Comedy of Errors finally ended, Mike was located, and he was safely delivered back to the care home, albeit a day late. Since then, Mike's health has been up and down. Some days he has been in good spirits, whereas other days he has been heartbreakingly sad or lost or languid. On Father's Day, I could barely keep him awake long enough to look at his cards, yet staff told me when I visited tonight that he had sat and watched the World Cup yesterday evening.

It's the staff that has given me lots to think about.

When this particular care home was suggested, I'd never heard of it and just worried about how far away it was. However, I was in a bad way mentally and so I agreed to send him there. Prior to then, I had always visited places and Mike had tried them out before I would allow him to stay there. I suppose it's a testament to just how low I'd become when I agreed to Mike going there regardless. Vicky told me that I could move him if I didn't like it, but that I really needed the break. I agreed.

Before all this happened, Mike, Fred and I had visited a small care home just down the road from us, and we all liked it. I had decided that, if Mike had to go into a home permanently, then this was where I wanted him to be, so that he would be just down the road from me, at all times, when the time came, sometime in the future.

But that future has come running straight at me, full pelt, threatening to bowl me over.

My view has had to change. Since Mike has been in respite this time, I have come to terms with the fact that I can't cope with him at home now. If I get a grant for a new wet room and I create a bedroom downstairs, he can come home, but these things take time.

While talking to Jo at the home on Sunday, I got very emotional at the thought of Mike coming home and me not being able to manage his considerable needs. I also got upset at the thought of him not coming home at all. She was very calming and suggested that Mike stay until there was space in the care home near us.

This isn't a decision akin to: shall I have the flapjack or the brownie? This is more like: shall I continue to struggle and get upset looking after the man I vowed to love and cherish in sickness and in health, or shall I abandon him and live forever after with the guilt?

I've never been a decision-maker.

I had a lovely visit with him in the home this evening. He was alert, funny and loving, and we were soon laughing together. The day staff went off duty, bidding Mike goodnight. He said to me: "They're a good bunch." Then the night shift arrived, greeting Mike like a long-lost friend, and he seemed pleased to see each and every one of them. It was heart-warming to see him comfortable with them, joining in their banter, and they told me that he'd had a good night's sleep the night before. The continuity of his care is comforting. Of course, they're attractive young ladies asking him if he wants a shower in the morning. Why would he want to come home?

I think I'm coming to the decision to let him stay there indefinitely, even though it's not that close to home: he's happy and safe, and I like the staff. Spending quality time with him is paramount, and I seem to be able to do that there, although I wish they had a settee so that we could have a proper cuddle.

Last week, when I was talking to my friend, Toni, I was telling her that there is a time when things are totally normal between Mike and me. That time is when he's asleep in bed and I finish doing the vitally important end of day chores: checking Facebook, playing Ruzzle, shopping on Ebay. When I finally turn off the light and settle down, Mike subconsciously lifts his arm for me to lay on his chest and he cuddles me. As I go to sleep, it's just me and my husband, loving each other, Alzheimer's temporarily forgotten.

And this is why, although I know it's for the best and that Mike is being well cared for, I can't bear the thought that he will never sleep in our bed again.

Once the decision had been made to let Mike stay at the home and I came to terms with the fact that he wasn't coming back to me, a new chapter of routine began. The main centre where I taught and where I had a desk for the coordination side of my role was in Wigston, so it was convenient for visiting straight from work. I went nearly every day and phoned when I couldn't. I even went after my class finished at 9pm as Mike was still up. One of the occasional residents who was physically fragile but mentally sound and who used to book herself into the home when her daughter was unavailable said to me: "Are you here again?" She was used to most of the residents getting weekly visits, if that. She said: "You must be Cathy. He calls for you when you're not here."

Have I told you lately that I love you?
30th June 2018

I just got in from a visit to the care home and hugged my Mike-replica, Fred, and let him comfort me while I sobbed. I told him that his dad would always live on because of him and his siblings. Fred was being the grown up while I crumbled under the enormity of what I have lost, despite having foolishly told people today how well I was coping.

I met up with a lot of colleagues today whom I only see three or four times a year. It was our summer conference at the Leicester Tigers rugby ground. The sun was shining, the speaker was entertaining, and the tea was plentiful; I was feeling upbeat, and some commented on how well I looked. It made me feel strong that I was being seen to be coping with my dire situation.

With the handful of colleagues who are also friends, I was pragmatic, explaining that I was lucky to have had 25 quality years of marriage with my best friend before dementia struck: some couples never find the level of happiness that we achieved for so long.

However, later, in the garden at the care home, I broke.

Mike and I were having a lovely time under the gazebo; I was trimming his beard and moustache, having just shaved his cheeks and neck, and given him a manicure. I've gotten into a routine with this: it passes the time, keeps Mike looking tip top and gives him the feeling of being pampered. I keep a bag in the car with me with the tools needed. Putting cream on his dry skin is another necessary but loving activity that makes visits intimate and productive.

When I finished, I got my phone out and Googled: Have I told you lately that I love you? by Van Morrison. When we got married in 1990, our first dance was to Groovy Kind of Love by Phil Collins and it's still "our song" but Van Morrison's gruffly intoned ballad overtook our wedding song in its importance somewhere along the way. Mike would ring me up in the middle of the day from work and tell me to turn the radio on to a particular station because it was playing. If we were together when either of those songs came on, we always danced, whether we were in the kitchen or the stable.

So, when my iPhone suddenly started playing the familiar introductory piano riff, Mike put his arms in the air and declared: "I love this song!" then cuddled me up to him and sang along. Halfway through the instrumental part, tears streaming down my face, he looked at me, right at me, and really saw me and said: "I love you," with a huge emphasis on the middle word.

With everything else stripped back, we are still two people who love each other deeply.

We played other songs and enjoyed the outdoors, and each other, and then I settled him back in the main lounge. By the time I had gone to fetch my bag from the garden, Mike was nodding in the high-backed chair. We exchanged farewells and loving words and I let myself out.

I made it to the car before I started to cry for my loss, for my wonderful husband and for my soulmate, with big, wracking, ugly sobs.

Yes, now that Mike is in a home, I can enjoy quality time with him again; I can regain my role as his wife rather than his carer but now that I'm not getting frustrated and upset by my inability to cope for his complex needs, I'm able to remember and to mourn for the life we had, which is gone forever.

Some people are unlucky enough to understand more than others what the Alzheimer's journey is like. One of these sent me a lovely letter that I turned into a blog post.

Letters from the heart
8th July 2018

I have a good friend, my twin, (I'll explain later) who lives in Florida. Wayne was his mum's carer when she had Alzheimer's and has since been his 98-year-old D-Day veteran father's carer.

Since Mike was diagnosed with Alzheimer's, I have quietly written this blog, but it wasn't until this year that Wayne discovered it. I had never gone out of my way to publicise Mike's illness because he had presented so well that it was hidden for four years. Indeed, three years ago, when Wayne and I celebrated our 50th birthday with a food fight in the village hall, even with my American "twin's" experience of Alzheimer's, he didn't spot the signs.

Now that it's out in the open, Wayne's support and understanding is immeasurable.

Although we were born a day and a continent apart, Wayne and I consider ourselves twins. We celebrated our 45th together in Florida, and our 50th here. We have a couple of years to go before we decide what to do for our 55th.

We met in Paris in strange circumstances in 2000 when the Channel Tunnel had been closed because of a mudslide. It was one of the very few times that I hadn't driven myself to see Christiane in Amiens (See my post: Bittersweet). Instead, Mike had taken Fred and me to Ashford and deposited us at the Eurostar check in. Fred was just a baby and I think I remember needing the parental influence that Christiane has always given me, especially since losing my own mum and dad.

I had delayed my voyage home by a day as we had heard on the news that the Channel Tunnel was shut. It was lovely to spend an extra night with Christiane and, going a day later, I thought, would have cleared the backlog of travellers trapped by the mudslide. However, when I alighted the Amiens train in Paris, I was met by a wall of people waiting to board the Eurostar. Massive queues had formed and even the French were queuing in a very British manner.

I duly joined one of these queues and waited. Fred was asleep in his pushchair. I could see more travellers in the distance on a floor above and wondered how long it would take to get to that coveted queue on the last stretch.

Two hours later, we had moved about ten feet!

Human survival instinct kicking in, I found myself bonding with the passengers around me. We formed a group and became temporary best friends forever, strategically placing cases, rucksacks and Fred in his pushchair in a way that built a little fortress around the six or seven of us, that stopped people from cutting through our part of the queue. We moved forward, imperceptibly, as one. There was an American, a Japanese girl and I think the rest of us were English.

I was so pleased that Fred was asleep, and I wondered how I was going to cope when he woke up as there would have been no way he would have stayed put once awake and running round.

I needn't have worried.

When Fred eventually woke, I held him in my arms while my fellow clique members made a fuss of him. I had only had him in my arms for a few minutes when we were suddenly surrounded by several gendarmes, asking me how many were in my party. I told them it was just Fred and me. One of them picked up the pushchair, still set up for occupation, with bags dangling from the back, lifted it above his head and started to move away, telling me to follow. I bent down to pick up my case but so did the American. He said, quietly, "Do you want some help?"

"You can try," I replied, before standing up again.

The American took my case and his own bag and, surrounded by the other gendarmes, we bid a hasty goodbye to our friends, and followed the pushchair.

We were led past hundreds of people who were all staring daggers at us, some making unkind comments in English and in French about needing a baby to jump the queues. Once past all these people, we were taken up the stairs to the floor I'd seen from afar, which was also crammed with people queuing.

I thought we would join the back of one of these lines, only to find we were being escorted straight past them to the passport control. The original gendarme looked suspiciously at the American and asked me again how many were in my party. At this point I completely forgot that I was fluent in French and was unable to understand him. He shrugged, probably Gallically, and left us to it, while I innocently asked the American if he had his passport as it wasn't with mine and Fred's; it was an Oscar-winning performance.

From there we went straight on to the train, which was full of children and the elderly. Had Fred been awake and visible when we first entered the station, we would have been whisked straight through. You live and learn.

The American stored my case, sat down next to me, proffered his hand. and said, "Hi, I'm Wayne!" and that was the beginning of a wonderful friendship.

The following words are to me, from Wayne.

Hi Cathy

Yes, I completely understand (coping). Without Dad helping there is no way I could have cared for Mom on my own. Still, even with his help, I managed to get a bleeding stomach ulcer and came very close to a nervous breakdown.

During her last year, I found myself saying, "Well soon, when she is gone, Dad and I will be able to get out and enjoy life more." Of course, even as I was thinking those thoughts, I felt guilt-ridden and like a horrible person.

I was holding her in my arms when she finally did pass. I felt her last breath slip away. In that moment, I didn't feel relief or great sadness but an overwhelming sense of peace. Mom was no longing suffering. She could finally rest, be with God and her parents. Although I don't believe she ever suffered physically, I could never be sure inside how much she really knew about what was going on but could no longer communicate.

For the last two years, she was a shell of herself. I had to hand feed her breakfast, lunch, and dinner. She would walk but only if I stood behind her and looped my arms under hers to hold her up. In the bathroom, I held her up while Dad cleaned her. Rarely did she say anything. In her last year, I don't think she said more than six words. But every once in a while, when I was feeding her, she would look at me and say, "Thank you."

These moments were few and precious and, to this day, even now, bring tears to my eyes.

Since she has passed, Dad and I have been able to live and do more: we swam with dolphins; we travelled to Ireland twice, France once and Mexico several times; we also did several road trips here in the USA, visiting with family, old friends, and seeing new places. And while we have had fun, always something was/is missing. Especially for Dad.

Now sadly and unfortunately, I am starting to see him slowly slip away.

Our last road trip, a couple of weeks ago, was to the National D-DAY Memorial for the 74th anniversary of D-Day. In the pictures I took, you will see Dad smiling and happy. And for the most part he was. For a 98-year-old he did really great overall. But what you won't see in the pictures is me getting up with him 5 or 6 times a night to use the toilet. Sometimes he would walk there, and I'd have to help so he didn't fall, other times I would just give him the bedside urinal we brought, and I'd dump it myself. What you don't see is me getting angry and frustrated because, at 3:00am, he just wet himself after using the urinal twice within the last half hour, and then feeling guilty for getting so angry. What you don't see is, while we are driving, him repeatedly asking me the same question every twenty minutes. The pictures don't show you how, on the way home, he was confused about where "home" was and kept thinking we were going to his childhood home in Pittsburgh. There have been many more instances of him either confusing things, forgetting things, having a totally different take on a conversation we had with someone, or just plain giving me grief because I took one night out of the week to do something for myself. Or his headaches. I haven't even mentioned his headaches! These types of things I know you are all too familiar with. Most people see Dad during the day or when we go out to eat. These are the times he is up and full of energy. They don't see what it sometimes takes to get him to that point. Really, I guess I should not complain because, overall, he is still doing pretty well. I know I'm very lucky to still have my father in my life. It's just that I see him declining more and more and I'm afraid I know all too well where it's heading. Again, I find myself thinking about the day Dad is gone and I can finally have my life back, and I immediately feel like that same horrible person and am wracked with guilt.

We are planning a big party for him, for his 99th this September. Hopefully some of his nieces and nephews will be able to attend. To top off all of Dad's issues, last Sunday, on Father's Day, I noticed a bump on his head. Turns out, it wasn't a bump but shingles! Fortunately, he is not in any pain. However, for the last few days he has had less energy and has been eating less. I'm hoping it's just the shingles and that, once he's over it, he'll pick back up a little more. Otherwise, I'm having serious doubts there will even be a 99th. Still, I will be optimistic, plan his party and even make reservations to return to the D-day Memorial next year for the 75th!!! After all, Dad is a pretty stubborn, cantankerous old man.

I wish I could come to Europe, but my travel days are pretty much on hold for now. I would invite you here but I'm afraid I really would not have time to do too much with you, unless you didn't mind a 98-year-old tagging along. As it is, I've really cut back on work. I no longer take new clients and, several times, have had to cancel on current ones. Fortunately, they all seem to understand.

Well, I know you really weren't expecting such a long reply from me, and I don't know if I've been much help. I think I mainly just needed to talk to someone else myself. I've been meaning to phone you so many times but, when I seem to have the time, it's always the middle of the night for you. Just know that, although each of our particular circumstances is a little different, I do understand the struggles you are going through, the fears, the loneliness, and the guilt you are experiencing.

Alzheimer's sucks.

I wish I could be there to give you a big hug and have a beer with you. Just know that I am thinking of you and, if you ever want to chat, I'm here.

Love,

Wayne

I have a shockingly bad memory and would have forgotten many of the upsets during our Alzheimer's journey had I not written them down. I rely on photos and family to remind me of past happenings and, since the advent of Facebook, I also rely on their "Memories" facility.

On this day five years ago
20th July 2018

Thanks to the *on this day* feature of Facebook, I am reminded daily of memories of my past. Today was poignant because it reminded me that, 5 years ago, we were in Tenerife at the start of a fabulous holiday, Mike sitting with his fingers in his ears so that he didn't have to listen to the welcome talk. It was a great holiday because we worked hard to make it so. We made the best of everything possible. Because, a few days earlier, Mike had been diagnosed with "some form of dementia."

At that stage, it was just poor memory, losing words and mild confusion (a bit like the morning after a good night at the Elephant and Castle) and I knew so little about dementia that I had no idea what we were facing. Looking back, life was still pretty perfect then.

We were yet to face the upset of Mike no longer being allowed to drive; his inability to change a plug, even though he had previously rewired houses; the missing massive chunks of his memory; his loss of ability to cook, or even to make a cup of tea; his frustration; his tears; his paranoia; his limitations when taking part in activities; his need for day care and then constant supervision; his gradual diminishing of dignity; the respite; and, finally, the permanent care home.

What a difference five years can make.

I've made similar comments before but, in retrospect, the stages of Alzheimer's are easy to see and to categorise. But when you are facing it, sitting on a balcony in Tenerife under a blue, blue sky, trying to get as much enjoyment out of every minute as possible, drinking in the sights and sounds as Mike was, as if he would never get the chance again, the future is unknown and scary.

I'm looking forward to Facebook memories over the next few days, to relive a time of love and laughter that heralded the beginning of the end.

Reflections – 2022

Life in the home became normal. As a regular visitor, I was given the door code to let myself in and was included in the tea round. Mike was mobile and able to feed himself and was a favourite among staff and residents.

Green-eyed monster

22nd July 2018

I'm assured that it is perfectly normal in a relationship to resent, dislike and even fear past partners. I'm no different. I remember feeling acutely jealous when Mike talked about "Ruthie" from his past. Even though she was firmly in the past and living her life by the time Mike and I met, I hated the fact that he still used her pet name. "Her name is Ruth!" I used to think.

The difference between me and others, however, is that Mike was seeing "Ruthie" before I was born!

There are 19 years between Mike and me. For the most part, age is just a number, but some facts about our age gap can be quite odd. For example, when I was 7 and wondering who my future husband would be, (we all did it) he was in fact married and celebrating the birth of his first son, Simon: freaky!

Mike always thought it was hilarious that I became jealous when he talked about the girls he'd known when he travelled the world in the Merchant Navy. He'd lived a big chunk of his life before I was old enough to be considered wife-material, so obviously he had racked up quite a number of conquests and a couple of wives prior to our becoming acquainted.

I needn't have worried; my man has been faithful to me for the past 30 years and I've not had any grounds for releasing the green-eyed monster lurking under my surface.

Until now...

It seems my husband is quite a hit with the ladies in residence!

In a recent post, I bemoaned the fact that there was no sofa to cuddle up on with Mike, only individual high-backed chairs, but then I discovered another lounge which did in fact contain a much-coveted two-seater settee. It is lovely to be able to snuggle up together; I can put my head on Mike's chest while he curls his arm around my shoulders: perfect...

Except that I rarely get a chance! I almost have to queue. My husband has an entourage.

Very often now, I turn up to visit Mike, only to find him on said settee with another woman. Can you believe it? And it's a different one every time! The ladies tend to gravitate towards Mike, and he seems quite accommodating. One of them even asked me: "Do you think he likes me?" as I squeezed on to the tiny slice of remaining seat next to my husband. I assured her that he probably did, and she seemed happy with that. I then waited until she left the room so I could jump into the vacated seat to reclaim my property.

There is a lovely Russian resident who forgets to speak English and who unashamedly kisses my husband in front of me. Mike seems resigned to the loud smacking kisses, first on his hand, then his head and then his mouth, which suggests that it may be a regular occurrence when I'm not there. "Excuse me, that's my husband," I say to no avail.

I often arrive and find Mike chatting to a lady and, unlike my younger, green-eyed self, it now makes me very happy to see him doing so. I've had a lot of good visits just recently, sometimes staying for up to three hours because we are enjoying each other's company; knowing that Mike isn't sitting and pining for me the whole time when I'm not there and could even be flirting with one of the staff or one of the female residents makes me feel content and accepting of the fact that he is now in the best place for his needs.

It isn't always so; I don't want to give the false impression that Mike's life is a bed of roses. He is still sometimes upset, lost, confused, frustrated and tearful but it certainly isn't the norm. Much like a factory displays how many days it has been without an accident, I count how many good visits I have with Mike on the trot. I got up to nine before an infection brought him down and I was faced with a totally different man. At the moment though, I'm on a run of five again which is brilliant.

So, jealous wife? Not anymore. I had Mike's best years all to myself and, now that I can't be with him constantly,

I'm grateful to anyone who makes him happy and brings out his lovely smile.

Reflections – 2022

All of a sudden, Mike forgot how to walk. Until that point, he had been extremely mobile around the home, walking up and down the corridors and changing sitting rooms regularly, able to walk into the dining room for meals completely unaided. From then on, he had to be moved around in a wheelchair and it severely impeded his quality of life. However, on occasions, his brain must have kicked in and allowed him to walk as staff would find him in a different chair from the one that they had left him in. This is mentioned in the next blog entry.

A bientôt, Papa
2nd October 2018

Fred went back to university this weekend, so he wanted to see his dad before he went. He was really keen to see him before going back to Reading because the deterioration has become increasingly rapid, and he realised that there may be a massive change by Christmas.

Now, let me explain something here, Fred is a little germophobic and a bit OCD (his siblings would say, "a lot"). Usually, when Fred goes to see his dad, he manages not to sit on anything that he thinks might not be as hygienic as he would like, and he is very careful as to what he touches. I'm sure he has practised breathing through his ears for when he's in the home, for fear of picking up a deadly, plague-like killer-microbe. But he was adamant that he wanted to see Mike and was mentally prepared.

However, when we got to the home, there was a sign on the door saying that there was a sickness and diarrhoea bug and that visitors should stay away unless it was urgent. Fred recoiled from the sign as if he'd been bitten, and elected to stay in the car, a look of pure panic on his face. We were assured that the bug was now under control and that the sign was just a precaution. We reminded Fred, as he begged for the car keys, that it was he who had wanted to see his dad before the new term began, so he reluctantly came in and stood uncomfortably in the middle of the room, making sure that he touched absolutely nothing, barely moving in case stirring up the air might alert some pernicious germ as to his presence. Happily, he was rewarded for his efforts with a: "How are you doing, son?" which was lovely and I'm sure Fred will take a lot of comfort from that, but he was struggling just to be breathing the same air as those who may or may not have the 'lurgy'.

Fred told me, while I was feeding Mike fruit and sharing the fork, that if I caught the bug, he would padlock me in my bedroom until I was well. I later heard him say that *he* was okay because he hadn't actually touched anything with his body and that he was going to burn his shoes when he got home!

The visit with Mike was wonderful. The fact that he recognised Fred made it all worthwhile. It was a joy to see him so happy and I'm sure that Fred will now go off to university secure in the knowledge that his dad knows him and wishes him well. He was making jokes; he was smiling and laughing; he is apparently eating well, and he looked clean and tidy. He did ask Fred, at one point, why he was holding his genitalia and Fred, who was in fact standing as if he were facing a Ronaldo direct freekick, replied, "You never know when you're going to be attacked." This made Mike guffaw.

Mike was eating fruit like it was going out of fashion. He started with grapes and then went on to pineapple as I had taken some in for him. He enjoyed the pineapple immensely, but I was worried that the huge amount of fruit that he had consumed would manifest as diarrhoea and the staff would think that he had the bug.

As usual, hallucinations were rife. Mike could see something on his fingers that he kept trying to shake off and he could see something just behind us that he said was really funny, so we all laughed together.

Although Mike still wasn't standing up, we heard from the staff that they had been finding him in a different chair when they came back into the room, so he must be able to stand and move when he is not thinking about it. (This is something I witnessed myself this evening, finding him midway across the lounge, albeit slowly and limping. He then walked with me into the dining room - result!)

Before this visit, I believed that Mike was at what I had feared was stage six of the seven stages of Alzheimer's, because of his inability to walk and toilet properly. However, on the strength of this particular visit, I think he is back at stage five, which means that I can still enjoy his company and be his wife, albeit in a much-changed format from when I married him.

_____

_____

As of today, I live on my own
22nd October 2018

When Mike went into his care home in June, it was originally for two weeks' respite; it wasn't meant to be forever. However, as previous posts have explained, things conspired to keep him in there and that is now his permanent residence.

At the time of Mike's respite Fred was home from his second year at Reading University for the summer, albeit flitting back and forth between here and Coventry where his girlfriend lives, so the house always had that "lived in" feel. Indeed, Fred's choice of course (philosophy) means that he gets even longer at home in the summer than some of his friends, so when Mike's stay became officially "permanent", I knew I still had until the end of September to get myself ready for having the house to myself (if you don't count the four whippets and two cats!)

As the time loomed for Fred to leave, I was thrown a lifeline in the shape of a friend of ours from France, who was supposed to be a houseguest for a couple of weeks, but who ended up stranded here while Saab specialists endeavoured to locate, recondition, and fit a "new" engine to replace the one that blew up on the Coventry bypass. By the time the car was released, it was time for me to go on holiday, so I never did have to spend any time here on my own.

Skip forward a week and it's finally happened: I live alone.

It's never happened before; I have never lived in a house on my own; I went straight from living with my parents to having my own family. When Fred first went to university, Mike and I rattled around the empty nest a bit, but we got used to it. As the Alzheimer's progressed, I found myself looking forward more and more to the end of term. Fred provided company, comic relief, animal care, constant cups of tea and Daddy Day-care. The payback was me simply putting up with total and utter devastation of the kitchen and bathroom on a daily basis. Well worth it.

I returned from my brother's house in Spain this lunchtime and have felt unbearably sad, not as if I've just had a lovely holiday. The realisation of my new status as of today is leaving me feeling almost bereaved, although my visit to Mike this evening proved that to be untrue. We spent a lovely hour-and-a-half together, once most of the more demanding residents had been taken to bed, eating cake, drinking tea and looking at Mike's new BBC Wildlife magazine that had been delivered while I was away. Mike was happy, friendly, and funny. It was most enjoyable.

But then I got home. Just having to keep all the doors locked is a new experience and turning all the lights out before bed takes on a whole new feeling when there is nobody else in the house, especially as I finished listening to my talking book today on the plane: Sleepers' Castle by Barbara Erskine. Her writing is enough to terrify me even in a crowd!

I'm now in bed. I can't hear anyone moving around the house and, as I have nobody to talk to, I decided to tell you. Thank you for reading my post and keeping me company on my first night alone.

_____
_____

Reflections – 2022

Living alone gave me lots of time for reflection and regrets. My notebook became full of short, sad thoughts as they happened.

A thought
27th October 2018

Alzheimer's is an evil illness. Looking back is when you notice the speed of the deterioration. You don't notice its insidious seeping into every pore of its victim until it's measured by "last year he could do this"; "last month he could do that"; "last week he was able to do the other."

I'm now measuring Mike's deterioration in weeks.

I was bitter about my mum dying at 69, until Mike started to suffer this hell. I'm so glad she didn't have to go through it. My heart goes out to anyone suffering this with loved ones.

Mike had a bad experience with a chicken when he was a teenager (don't ask) and he wouldn't eat it if it tasted like chicken. If I disguised it with plenty of spices and other flavours, he was ok. When I dished up chicken for dinner one Sunday, Mike's mum, who was visiting, told me:

"Michael doesn't eat chicken."

"He eats my chicken," I told her smugly.

Mike and his brothers all disliked lamb too, due to the fatty neck that their mother used to dish up for them when they were young. Despite lamb being a favourite of my mum's, I rarely bought it as Mike was just not a fan (unless cooked by Christiane!)

When we went to catered events, Mike would often order the vegetarian option for fear of being served chicken or lamb, and he wasn't keen on fish either. His signature dish that he cooked on a Saturday for years to give me a day off from the kitchen was spaghetti Bolognese. Everyone who ate with us on a Saturday over the years loved it, especially Aunty Grace who came to live with us for six months after having been hospitalised with hypothermia. She'd never eaten spaghetti before, so we had to cut hers up for her. She tucked into it with relish.

When Mike was settled into the home, I often arrived at mealtimes so that I could help to feed him, and it soon became clear that he would eat whatever was put in front of him, even chicken or fish. I said nothing, obviously, but he had clearly forgotten that he was a fussy eater, unless it came to pudding – he was a big pudding-eater when we went out, but I rarely served up a dessert.

I used to take sweet treats into the home for Mike, things that he loved, but by then he would have eaten anything!

Out of Control
24th November 2018

One Monday morning in April at the end of the '80s, I stood outside the school gates and watched in despair as our rising 5-year-old son, Joe, joined the wrong queue in the playground to enter the building for his first day. It was my first experience of helplessness. For nearly five years, every second of every day of Joe's life had involved me or his grandparents. All of a sudden, I was powerless. The urge to run in and guide him to the right line was enormous, but my time as his main influence had come to an end.

It's similar to how I'm feeling with Mike, only in reverse. In Joe's nearly 5 years, he progressed rapidly up to the point where I relinquished control. I had, however got him to a point where he could manage without me.

For Mike's last 5 years, he has declined, slowly at first, then faster and now as rapidly as Joe progressed. This dystopian version of the wonderful time I spent with Joe is a mirror image. Mike hasn't yet got to the totally helpless stage of baby Joe, but I know it's coming.

In the '80s, I loved my role as Mum. I have never regretted having Joe, despite the less-than-perfect circumstances, and I embraced my new life with joy and enchantment. Having responsibility for a human being's life is an honour and a privilege. However, when that responsibility involves controlling a grown up, acting as his memory, ensuring he takes his tablets, driving him everywhere, holding him a prisoner, and, during the last year, keeping him clean, it's no longer a privilege; it's a duty.

For the past two years, every waking moment (and some sleeping ones too) I have had to think of how my activities would fit in with Mike: exactly like life with a young child. I remember handing him his inhaler which he took without a word, so I said: "What do you say?" as if he were my child.

His reply was: "Stuff your inhaler!" which was more like the Mike I know and love.

When he was in respite care in a home in Enderby, and indeed when he was first in the Wigston home (as it was only supposed to be temporary, emergency respite) I still controlled his medication, timetable, and diet.

Now that Mike is a permanent resident, I watch on from the side lines while others make decisions for him, decide his medical treatment, create his routine and shape his life.

I've not been able to see this change as a relief. Some people believe I must feel this way after having had every waking thought tied to considerations of Mike: "It must be a relief for you now that he's being looked after," but no, it isn't. Relief is the wrong emotion. Instead, I feel sad, lost, guilty, unneeded, useless, surplus-to-requirements, redundant, without purpose.

Since Mike has forgotten how to walk, I can't even take him to the toilet or for a shower anymore. I have to ask the staff. The girls have to work in pairs as they need the help of a mechanical standing aid to get him into a wheelchair. Then, when they return him to me, clean and fresh, he greets me anew, having forgotten that he'd seen me ten minutes before.

Earlier this week came the day I was dreading: he didn't remember me. I'm used to him calling the staff, "sweetheart," "love" and "dear", and I'm pleased he feels comfortable with them. However, yesterday it was bittersweet to hear just after he'd asked who I was.

I consoled myself with the intonation of his question. Instead of asking, "Who are *you*?" with the emphasis on "you", he asked, "Who *are* you?" with the stress on "are." To my mind, this shows he knew me but couldn't work out how he knew me, rather than viewing me as a total stranger. And it only took a couple of minutes before he realised who I was, so I'm not getting too down about it.

I hope my blog helps people who are not so far along their Alzheimer's journey to enjoy as much of their lives as possible. When I look back, things that were upsetting or stressful two years ago were far less stressful than how things were a year ago. Despite the many problems and upsets a year ago, it was so much better when I had control.

There came a time when Mike stopped calling for me, and fretting that I wasn't there, so I started visiting every other day, instead of every day, although I always spent Friday evening with him.

Just a normal Friday... Not!
9th December 2018

If I were to tell you that, last night, Mike and I enjoyed an evening of cabaret with singing and clapping and laughter, and an adoring crowd of fans, you would be forgiven for thinking that I'd broken him out of the home and run away to the city. However, the fun and frivolity we had was all in situ.

There is a new resident who was part of a well-known band from the '70s; he was easily Googled. The staff was clearly star struck as they sat around his circular table, laughing at his jokes, and urging him to play for them.

I sat at a nearby table with Mike. I had been trying to get him to engage with me: it sometimes takes a while to bring him back from Alzheimer's World where he spends most of his time. When I had first got to the home, he had seemed very distracted, parked in his wheelchair next to the window. He was pulling at the curtains and didn't react to me until after I had given him a shave. Of course, snagging his beard with the electric shaver and pulling out facial hair by the roots is quite a good way of getting his attention but it's not textbook.

After this, he looked at me for quite some time without really realising who I was. Even seeing me with a cup of tea didn't do much to jog his memory. I played him some music on my phone, the usual stuff he reacts to:

Dam Busters, Deacon Blue, Only Fools and Horses, but it wasn't until I played Somewhere Out There by James Ingram and Linda Ronstadt that I got him back. Ironically, it's a song that he himself decided long ago, long before Alzheimer's, that he wanted to have played at his funeral. It's one of our special songs and it got through to him. He looked at me and saw me, and then he reached out and touched my face. My Mike was back in the room.

Shortly after that, the staff managed to persuade the new resident, Tim, (not his real name for obvious reasons) to fetch his guitar. He agreed on the proviso that the staff would all sing. They all agreed and set about Googling the lyrics to his songs. None of them was old enough to remember him in his 70's heyday, the majority not even born until 20 years later. The band was very well known when I was a young girl and they often played in the Croft Club, just down the road from where I grew up, so I was most interested to hear him play and sing.

Amid much hilarity, Tim tried to teach the girls to add in the typically 70's "Do-wop-di-wop" backing bits. I was singing along and enjoying myself, nostalgically, when Mike started to tap the table in time to the music. In fact, when Tim started to play songs by other artists and set off on a rendition of My Generation, Mike sat up in his chair and started briefly to sing along. Tim kindly played the song again when I made it known that Mike had reacted so well to it and the staff turned their gazes to watch Mike "boogie". I was as proud of him as a young mum showing off a new-born's first attempts at smiling.

It was a really lovely evening full of laughter and songs and I felt like I'd been out on a date with my husband.

Obviously, there were all the usual distractions that happen regularly in the home. There's the lady who comes to tell us animated anecdotes but forgets that we can't speak Russian, although, scarily, Mike sometimes seems to understand her perfectly; then, there are those who while away the evening by trying to get out of the building, occasionally via the windows; others have their own specialities, such as stealing sandwiches and setting off the fire alarms (thankfully not during this particular evening).

Afterwards, I had a chat with the singer who is at the very early stages of his illness and who sympathised with me over Mike's Alzheimer's. He shook Mike's hand and asked him, "Who is this lovely young lady?" (meaning me, of course - keep up!) and, to my amazement and delight, Mike answered, "I'm not telling you. This is my wife." It really swells my heart when he shows that he knows who I am. He even said a few more full sentences to Tim that actually made sense, which is a rarity these days.

So, all in all, it was a very pleasant Friday evening in the home. Visits where I can enjoy Mike's company are wonderful and leave me happy, relaxed and with the impression that the world isn't so bad after all.

I was fortunate enough to take the afternoon off work, that coincided with an organised activity at the home. I had wanted to be with Mike, and it turned out to be a most interesting afternoon.

Arachnophobia

10th February 2019

See Cathy care for her husband, sitting with him, being with him, loving him.

Feel Cathy's depth of emotion for her husband, keeping his mind active, protecting him from his disease, showing her commitment to him.

Hear Cathy scream as a tarantula is dropped 3 feet away from her, all thoughts of caring for her poor husband out of the window, allowing only thoughts of self-preservation to register as her worst fear is realised!

It's funny how sheer terror can obliterate all good intentions. At that moment, I didn't care what happened to the world, Mike included, as long as that vile creature was taken away. It's lucky it didn't start running towards me or else the exotic pet handler would now be eight legs short in his menagerie.

I remember a similar occurrence happening around 30 years ago, whilst on holiday near Rocamadour. My dad was driving, and I was in the passenger seat, navigating.

All of a sudden, a massive spider came running across the dashboard, intent on killing me, obviously. I'm not quite sure of the order of events, but I ended up in the back of the car, landing ungracefully on my poor mum with her arthritic joints, and waking my fourteen-month-old son, Joe. Now, I never had knees that worked properly so I have no idea how I scrambled over to safety in my panic, but I clearly didn't care who got hurt, nor how much of a road hazard I was creating. Luckily, Dad was able to pull up at the side of the road, grab the monster, chuck it out of the window and set off driving again, (me still wedged between the baby seat and my mother) all without breaking a sweat. He later remarked: "I felt the bloody thing kicking in my hand!"

The funniest thing was that the whole pantomime had been observed by a French family, picnicking on a bank at the side of the road. They had watched this Renault 12 swerve to a halt, while a screaming madwoman vaulted over the back seat and the driver threw a spider out of the window. It has probably tainted their view of English people ever since.

Anyway, back to the present dilemma, I want to put things into perspective. I may not have rid myself of my arachnophobia in 30 years but, in the care home, at the time that I was screaming at the aforementioned eight-legged beast, I had a lapful of lizard, a snake circling my neck, a frog in my left hand and a millipede in my right so I'm not totally pathetic: I just don't do spiders.

However, apart from this minor catastrophe, the rest of the afternoon was wonderful, with all of the residents handling reptiles, rodents and rabbits. There was rather a dearth of staff at this point though, having conveniently remembered far more pressing tasks that awaited them, far away from the impromptu zoo.

Mike was delighted when the handler put a lizard on his lap. He petted it and stroked it and posed for a photo, although he did then forget that it was alive and started fiddling with its back leg while he looked around the room at all the other goings on. I kept a close eye on it and, whilst the miniature prehistoric animal didn't seem to mind its leg being twiddled and squeezed as if it were plastic, I minded. I thought it better to remove said animal before any harm came to it, so I adopted it as my lap lizard.

I'm so pleased that I chose to take that afternoon off from work. I didn't know about the visiting animals beforehand; it was sheer coincidence. It's not the way that Mike and I used to spend quality time together but it's making the best of things and finding enjoyment wherever possible. I have added this lovely memory to my collection and will cherish it.

Many people die **with** Alzheimer's, something else killing them before the evil disease can steal every single faculty. Those who sadly die **of** Alzheimer's have many horrible stages to suffer before they are at peace.

When Mike lost the ability to hold himself up in his chair, he could no longer be allowed to sit in the lounge with the other residents, for fear of falling out of the chair and injuring himself. This final chapter, with Mike confined to bed, was the worst of all, but I did all I could to keep him stimulated. His room looked like a teenager's bedroom as I had Blutacked photos of family, birthday cards and pages from the BBC Wildlife magazine on every wall. I insisted on having the radio on all day to keep him company, and I read to him when I was there, sometimes eliciting a response when I read out a word like Manchester or Stretford End. There was a big armchair in the room, and I would pull it right up to the edge of the bed so that I could sit in the chair with my legs on Mike's covers.

At this point, like a baby being excited by its own voice, Mike would make sounds: blowing raspberries, singing in opera fashion, shouting. One day, while he was laying there making all sorts of noises that the staff said they could hear all over the home, I poured him a drink of orange squash. The noise was continuous, but I managed to get in: "Would you like a drink?" He instantly stopped shouting and said, really quickly: "Yes, please," and I was able to get him to drink a whole glassful. He soon went back to his nonsense chatter, but he was happy.

Hard Habit to Break
18ᵗʰ March 2019

Let's face it, cards on the table, there is nothing left to laugh about.

I'm perceived as someone coping, on top of my game, having fun on holiday and at the pub.

I'm not.

The holidays and fun times are a way of recharging my batteries so that I can take another run up and shoulder-charge the disease that is eating away at my husband, stealing him bit by bit, and turning him back into the baby he once was.

At times, I can appear callous by the matter-of-fact way that I talk about Mike's illness, but that is just a coping strategy, a way of dealing with the regular, "How's Mike?" question.

"Up and down," I say.

"As well as can be expected at this stage of his illness," I say.

"Dying bit by bit before my eyes," I never say.

Mike is now spending most of his time in bed. He lost the ability to walk or stand several months ago but now he is unable to hold his own posture in a chair: hence bed rest. This means he has no conversations, arguments or spontaneous singing to grab his attention as he would in the lounge with the other residents. Nobody walks past, nobody sits next to him, nobody makes inane small talk with him.

The staff has a lot on. They go in regularly to change him, feed him, give him tablets, but they don't have time to sit with him and listen to his incoherent ramblings. When I'm there, I have "conversations" with him while I'm shaving him or cutting his nails or cleaning him up, but they're nonsensical. However, it's interaction and that keeps him engaged and, mainly, happy, so the content of the chat is irrelevant.

Mike was weighed during my visit a few days ago in a sort of hammock contraption. He weighs 7 stone 2 pounds! I can see that he is all skin and bone with my own eyes, but hearing the actual weight was quite a shock. I took a photo of him being weighed as he was being amenable.

I take photos of the good moments. This is mainly for my own benefit, but I'm also immensely proud of him when he achieves something unexpected, or when he smiles and reminds me of who he used to be. Unfortunately, it gives false hope to those who no longer see him and who, judging by the photos, think that the "old" Mike is still there.

For the most part, I control my emotions until I can indulge myself in private or with close family and friends. However, when the radio played "Hard Habit to Break" by Chicago when I was visiting the other day, I choked up. Luckily, Mike didn't notice. The poignant lyrics, "I guess I thought you'd be here forever," and, "Don't know what you've got until it's gone," had me blubbering into a small piece of tissue.

But then, yesterday, "Somewhere Out There," by James Ingram and Linda Ronstadt, played on the radio. This is a song, as I've mentioned previously, that Mike and I said we wanted played at his funeral. We had this conversation many, many years before Alzheimer's. When it got to the chorus, Mike thrust his fist into the air in appreciation of the music. It was a wonderful moment, not at all sad, that had me reaching again for my camera.

In their song, Chicago sang, "Being without you takes a lot of getting used to," but I'm not without him yet, and so I continue to document the good moments while I can.

But I spoke too soon.

Last Requests

13ᵗʰ April 2019

Mike always told me, when he was of sound mind and body, that, when the time came, he wanted some of "that blue stuff" that the vet injected into our old Labrador-cross, Sally, in 1995. My son's girlfriend has reliably informed me that the liquid is now pink, but the effect is the same: a dignified, painless, peaceful ending, surrounded by love. What I wouldn't give for a bit of pink juice right now.

Whilst in Poundstretchers yesterday afternoon, on the eve of my Easter holiday to France, having picked up my new glasses and feeling almost ready (apart from cleaning the house so that my friend who feeds my cats while I'm away doesn't think I'm a total slob), I got a call from Mike's care home. I was due at the home anyway, partly because I always go the day before I leave for holiday, partly because it was Friday, partly to adjust the radiator and install a fan (The carers are lovely but they aren't allowed to do maintenance work so I've been in every day, instead of every other day, to turn the water supply to the radiator off or on, depending on the weather) and partly because the home had rung earlier in the day to say that Mike was being given Oramorph and that the doctor had been requested.

The call from the home was so that the doctor could talk frankly to me. I spent the next 20 minutes pacing the bedding aisle while the doctor and I talked, and I fought valiantly to keep my voice steady and my tears inside. I managed to discuss DNAR (Do Not Attempt Resuscitation) as if I were sorting out car insurance. I then calmly cancelled my hair appointment and drove to the home. The doctor told me that there was no need to "floor it" to get to Mike's bedside, but that I should tell the family.

Our sons, Joe and Fred came to keep vigil with me well beyond midnight, the former having aborted a business trip to China (he made it as far as Heathrow but didn't board the plane), the latter accepting that he wasn't going to France and that he needed to stop thinking about packing. This morning, Vicky, is here with me, having flown in from Spain, and my boys are due back later.

If only we could give Mike the dignified end that Sally had, we would.

Reflections - 2022

During this three-day vigil, the inane sounds that Mike had been making for a few weeks had stopped, and he was doing nothing but stare. The staff had to turn him every two hours to avoid bed sores, so I was constantly rearranging the pictures on the wall so that he always had something in his line of vision. His hip had been a long-standing cause of pain ever since he had been in the home, and it was now locked in an unnatural position, so that it always jutted out and forced his right leg to cross his left. When the staff washed him, his hip was always painful but now, instead of shouting at his carers, and complaining that they were hurting him, he opened his mouth in pain, but no sound came out. It was heart-breaking to watch.

I spent two nights with him, the first on a camp bed with my hand holding his arm. The last night, when the carers turned him, I asked if they could move him over to the edge and push the bed to the wall. That way, I was able to sleep with him, although I had to be very careful not to hurt his hip. He looked at me during this time and I told him to, "let go," as I cuddled him. I'm glad I managed to spend the last night with my Mike.

The following day, we arranged the room so that we could put chairs all around the bed. The staff brought us an urn so that we could make our own tea, and many of the carers came for a few minutes to say goodbye to Mike.

Joe, Fred, Renée and Vicky were with me, and we were expecting James, who had been on holiday. He rang Vicky to ask if he had time to drop his wife and children off but his sister advised him to get there as soon as possible.

When James arrived, and after he had greeted his dad, we realised that, with so many of us, we were missing a cup so Joe went off to the kitchen to fetch one. He got back and we all took to our seats around the bed with cups of tea and biscuits. It was as if Mike had been waiting for us all to be there because, no sooner had we all sat down and I had taken a bite of my biscuit, Vicky said: "Cathy, you may want to put your cup down."

It was time.

I put my cup on the floor and leant over to put my head against Mike's head, ridiculously aware that I had a mouthful of biscuit. In hindsight, I should have spat it out, but I didn't, and I stroked Mike as he went to sleep, the last thing he would have heard was me crunching quietly. The kids all waited while I had my time with him, and then they all came and kissed and cuddled him. Joe tried to close Mike's eyes and jumped as a gasp came out of his dad's mouth, although Vicky assured us that this was normal.

There followed a couple of hours of strangeness for us all, never having been in this position before, while we waited for the undertakers. We didn't know whether to cover Mike up or not – what was the done thing? We finally decided that there was no rule book and that we could balance things on him like Jenga if we so chose, not that we did, so we covered him up. Humour became a coping strategy for us all.

When the undertakers arrived, they were surprised by my choice of venue for Mike's funeral as it was so far away from the home, but we assured them that it was close to where we lived. They asked us to wait downstairs while they did what they had to, and there followed a strange, what seemed to us as impromptu, ceremony, but which must happen every time there is a death in the home. The residents had been herded into the main lounge and the curtains pulled, and the majority of the staff lined the lobby on either side; we joined them to wait for the stretcher to be wheeled past and taken out to the waiting transport.

It was extremely emotional, and we all went out into the garden once Mike had been taken, and our grief overflowed. For some reason, we formed a circle, the six of us, comforting each other. Then, as we dried our eyes, we realised that we had formed this circle around a whole slice of cooked bacon. It must have been left over from breakfast and put out for the birds, but it was surreal and caused some mirth. Mike would have thought it funny too.

Life Goes On

22nd April 2019

I am watching my son, Fred, from the bathroom window of a 300-year-old farmhouse in Normandy. He is racing our whippets, timing them individually against each other with a stopwatch. Renée is at the starting point sending them off. I'm sure there is a lot of cheating or favouritism going on, much like when, as a child, my brother swore that he wasn't pushing the Jaguar any faster than his other Dinky cars.

I never knew Mike when he was approaching his 21st birthday; I didn't meet him until he was 42, but I should imagine he looked and behaved very much like the young man I'm watching out of the window now.

Fred was born when Mike was 52. He was aware that he was an old dad compared to Fred's friends' dads and he said he would be happy if he could just see his youngest child's twenty-first birthday.

He made it by all but 2 months.

Fred will be 21 in June and will be a philosophy graduate the month after. His dad won't be there for either. Fred is philosophical about this (obviously) and realises that Mike didn't "just" miss these occasions. He has been alive but not living for many months now.

Having spent so long caring for Mike, I am now able to remember the times that he cared for me, or that we cared for each other, and the good times in a long and extremely happy marriage. I haven't yet been strong enough to read the condolence cards and letters that people have kindly sent but I hope I will soon be able. The funeral plans are keeping things organised and business-like for now, but I am smiling again at photos of my healthy husband, instead of feeling sad. Hiding in France is probably putting off the inevitable sympathy that I have to face from those who also loved and cared for Mike, and that I know will release the floodgates of repressed emotion.

Having said that, I am already getting feelings of guilt: guilt that I didn't support football at all; guilt that I nagged when Mike was watching the match; guilt that I didn't understand his euphoria when his team scored. I feel guilty that I didn't share his enjoyment of Bob Dylan and encouraged him not to play it in the house when I was there. And, ultimately, I feel guilty that I wasn't able to find him a cure for Alzheimer's.

There will be Dylan aplenty at the wake, and a sharing of happy memories and funny stories to remember my wonderful man. Mike will have had his wish to be buried with Honey's dog tag which will have been attached to the plush toy whippet that was a Christmas present from his first-born. In the meantime, I am spending quality time with my mini-Mike, Fred. Watching him with our whippets gives me immense

134

happiness but I had better get on with the day and change out of my Manchester United pyjama bottoms.

Reflections – 2022

When Fred, Renée and I returned from France, real life began again. My first wish was to go and see Mike in the chapel of rest, which I actually did several times, wanting to spend as much time with him as possible.

The first time I went, I took all the sympathy cards and letters that I had received, not having been brave enough to open them before, so that I could read them to Mike. The lady on duty was extremely welcoming and made me two cups of tea during my visit, the second one offered once I had been there for a while and was obviously in no hurry to leave. I positioned myself at the head of the coffin where I could look along Mike's body from the top, imagining that he was just asleep. I avoided looking directly at his face as it was too "waxy" and not quite like him. I also made sure that, on the many occasions that I kissed him, it was on his lovely, thick head of hair, rather than his cold skin. His hair really was his crowning glory, much thicker and darker than most men of his age. He was positioned casually with his legs crossed, which of course was because of the way his hip had set but which looked relaxed to those who didn't know about the hip problems. In his arms, he held the plush whippet that my stepson had bought him, correctly adorned with Honey's name tag, as requested in the very first blog post. He was wearing his smart, brown, suede jacket, with the same shirt, tie and trousers that he had worn for my nieces' wedding, which was the last time he had dressed formally.

I read aloud all the messages and letters, working my way through the box of tissues that had kindly been provided, making comments and asides to accompany the condolences, just as if we were still in the home and spending time together. The whole experience was strangely comforting, albeit exhausting, and it took a while for the puffiness to leave my eyes.

The funeral was lovely. Some of it is a bit of a blur but I have been reminded of some important moments by the wonderful Order of Service created by Leah. I had totally forgotten that one of Mike's carers had written a poem, and I have no recollection of it being read out during the service by Vicky, but I am told that she read it really well. Here it is:

Remember Me

By Liz Poulton

Remember me as I used to be,

Not as you saw me last.

Think of the man you used to know

And remember me, well, in the past.

Remember me as I used to be,

So in love with my beautiful wife.

Remember the energy I used to have,

As we travelled our long-shared life.

Remember me as a family man,

So proud of each daughter and son.

Remember a grandad who loved you,

So quietly proud of each one.

Remember me as a handy man,

Was there nothing that I couldn't do?

Remember me as a friend in the pub,

Where we shared a pint... or two!

Remember me as I used to be,

So modest, so polite and so fine.

Arguing often that black was white,

And obviously right every time.

Remember me as I used to be,

And don't grieve for the man I became.

In your mind keep the person you used to know,

Feel my love as you mention my name.

Mike got his wish to enter the crematorium to the music of the 633 Squadron, carried by his four sons. We also listened to Somewhere Out There by James Ingram and Linda Ronstadt, as he had requested, and left the building listening to one of his favourite songs by Deacon Blue: Dignity. The reference to a boat in the song was a nod to Mike's time in the Merchant Navy, as was the hymn we chose to sing: Eternal Father, Strong To Save, which has the line "for those in peril on the sea". We had a Unitarian minister who gave a lovely eulogy, albeit slightly inaccurate at times and had people looking round to see who had come all the way from New Zealand for the funeral: nobody, but it was Mike's favourite country, having been there during his time at sea.

Mike's children arranged for a lovely floral tribute to be made. They contacted All Weather Windows where Mike had worked before he retired, and had a uPVC window made that was decorated with flowers by a local florist. This stood at the front of the crematorium during the service in recognition of Mike's many years in the window trade. In the congregation, there were several former colleagues, including the factory staff and window fitters who had collected together to give Mike a framed signed Bobby Charlton shirt for his retirement.

Inadvertently, after the service, once outside, a queue formed to hug me and give condolences. It was slightly surreal but, in retrospect, comical. I was reasonably calm and holding myself together, thanking everyone for their words, until a former racing competitor from the old days of FF2000 got to the head of the queue and told me how sorry he was. The enormity that someone from so long ago had travelled so far to pay their respects made me crumble and I burst into loud tears.

From then on, I was a wreck, even when neighbours and colleagues said nice things, blubbing like a baby.

Composure had returned by the time we got back to the Elephant and Castle for the buffet, and we had a really nice afternoon, reminiscing and laughing. My friend, Emma, took the book round for everyone to comment in and sign, and we even had a cause for celebration when my niece announced that she was pregnant. It was a poignant reminder that life goes on.

Later, the landlord apologised and said that the fortnightly quiz was about to start and that we could continue our wake in the back room. However, in true Pownall and Loynes fashion, we all formed ourselves into teams of four and took part. Mike would have loved it. I don't remember who won but I do remember the convivial atmosphere and the fact that Renée got a bit tipsy and took a lot of good-natured flak from her team members (Joe, James and cousin Duncan) for some of her funny nswers.

All in all, it was a fantastic send-off.

_____
_____

There followed a lot to sort out, paraphernalia to sign, accounts to alter, bills to pay, which kept me occupied in the early days, but mourning was well and truly taking place and I eventually needed the cathartic release of writing a blog post.

To cope or not to cope, that is the question
9th July 2019

When is the sell-by date? When people say, "You know where I am," how long does that last? How long is it valid for? Is there an expiry date?

People see me coping, laughing, going on holiday, working, living. They ask me how I am. When you ask somebody that, you mean in that moment, at that precise time when you've met in a corridor or at the shops, or at the pub. The expected reply, is, "Fine, thanks, are you?" That's all anyone ever expects. You don't ask somebody how they are and expect them to actually tell you about their sore toe or their disappointment over not having received a pay rise. They expect you to say fine. And that's what I say. But it isn't true. I'm fine in that minute, at that moment, in that instant. I'm fine when I'm at work, when I'm at the racetrack, when I'm busy. But I still have hours and hours to miss Mike, to wish he were still here, how he used to be, when he was still himself.

I lost my husband several years ago, but I was allowed to keep his body, albeit gradually breaking and crumbling apart. It was like a memorial. People have graves to visit when they lose someone. I had a life-sized replica of my husband as a memorial. But that memorial needed looking after, caring for emotionally, keeping clean, keeping presentable, keeping as active as possible, so that nobody saw that memorial and thought that, like an untended grave, it wasn't still loved, because it was: he was. I loved Mike until the day he died, and then I carried on loving the memory of him. And I miss him so much. And now that I am over the initial gratitude that he is no longer suffering, I realise the enormity of my loss.

Grieving takes on many roles. There is disbelief, there is sadness, there is anger, there is denial, there is acceptance; but when it's an Alzheimer's sufferer, the final stage after all that is death, and the whole grieving process has to start again, because he didn't really die the first time; it just seemed like it.

I went through a period early in 2018 when I didn't want to carry on anymore. My boys were self-sufficient, my husband was disappearing, and I felt I had lived my life. I was 53! And now I'm trying to live. I'm trying to find a future. But I'm spending most of my time in the past because I feel safe there.

A recent visit to Normandy for D Day has rekindled my interest in the part my dad played in World War II. I've spent so long researching World War I for the book that I've been writing for over 20 years that I never thought to consider what Dad had been through. I've discovered that I'm immensely proud of the part he played in our history. Having been at the commemorations for the 75th anniversary of D-Day, I would now like to trace Dad's army history, and to go to the Netherlands in September for the 75th anniversary of Arnhem. Dad was there! Then I would like to go to Norway next May for the 75th anniversary of the liberation of Norway as I have a framed certificate on my wall from Prince Olaf (later King Olaf) of Norway, thanking my dad (and many others) for liberating the country.

So, I'm submerged in the past, reliving my good memories of Mike and concentrating on history, and I'm planning my next holiday, and the one after that, and the one after that because that's the only way I can get through my todays. It's how I cope. It's how I avoid turning up on my friends' doorsteps in tears. My counsellor suggested this morning that I admit my grief to my friends instead of giving out the appearance of being "fine." Maybe.

I don't know how long the healing process is for losing a husband: I've never lost one before, and certainly never lost anyone while they were still alive. I know I still miss my mum and dad, who died in '96 and '98 respectively, but their deaths don't hurt me anymore and I can remember them with fondness, whereas I started hurting inside for Mike a couple of years before his death, as the Alzheimer's stole him, and I'm still hurting now. Despite my outward appearance of being fine, I'm not, and I don't know when I will be.

The First First
8ᵗʰ October 2019

Someone asked me the other day if I was still writing my blog and I didn't know what the answer was. I haven't written much since before Mike's funeral but there are still stories that I can tell and examples that may help other people in the same situation.

And there are still, I find, my own emotions to deal with; and this has been, by far, my most important reason for writing.

I went back to full time work almost immediately after Mike died, and I could talk about him and his death easily. My stepdaughter, Vicky, was the same, and we were both told we weren't grieving properly... (Where's the manual?)

I'm sure I appear to others as if I'm fine. I sometimes think I am too. I laugh, I look forward to things, I go on holiday. I'm learning to crochet with Renée, and I'm buying Peter Rabbit quilting magazines. I was able to be sympathetic to a colleague whose husband is terminally ill, without getting upset myself.

But then today, I went to the dentists', for a check-up. It used to be a six-monthly fun day out for me, as Mike and I got to spend a quality half hour in the waiting room, catching up with Joe and Fred. Today I was on my own as Fred was working and Joe makes his own appointments with my grandson, Felix. It hadn't occurred to me that it was my first check-up since losing Mike.

Everything went well as usual (I do have 32 teeth, you know) and then I went to the desk.

When I asked to book my next 6-monthly appointment. Fate, with its twisted sense of humour, put the words, "Tuesday the 14th of April," into the receptionist's mouth. The date was familiar, but I couldn't work out why. I was getting confused. Surely it hadn't been six months already since Mike died...

But it had. Almost 6 months to the day.

When I spluttered that I couldn't take that date because it would be the first anniversary of my husband's death, the receptionist's demeanour became more understanding, and less you-asked-for-six-months-and-there-are-others-waiting-so-just-let-me-write-your-card-and-you-can-pay-your-bill.

The senior receptionist, who has worked at the practice for years and has seen my boys grow up, overheard this conversation, and kindly voiced her sympathy. She said that she knew Mike had been poorly and was sorry for my loss. It completely knocked the breath out of me.

As I sat in the car park, regaining my composure, I thought about the time scale. When Joe and Fred had been growing up and visiting the dentist every six months, they made enormous leaps and strides in between each visit. Six months is a massive period of development for a baby, toddler, child and teenager, but I found out that it's also a massive period of decline for somebody with Alzheimer's. Mike's six-monthly leaps saw him just a little forgetful; then quite confused; then really confused and needing reassurance just to sit in the examining chair. Then one day, he didn't come with us at all because he was in a home, and the next time he didn't come was today because, six months ago, he left us.

The grief I felt today was raw, as if I had torn the scab off a wound that was healing nicely, and now it had to start all over again.

Today was my first visit to the dentist without Mike in my life. Tomorrow will be my first birthday without him. I wonder how that will go. Friends have apparently been expecting me to struggle with this, but I've already been remembering my 50th, five years ago, when I had a food-fight as my party, and Mike was there with me, chucking trifle and slipping on tuna sandwiches.

So yes, I think I will continue to write my blog, because I still have stories to tell, feelings to work through, advice to share and memories to enjoy.

However, my next blog post would be my last.

You don't get better; you get better at it
26th January 2020

Having just watched a programme about The Queen Mother, on the eve of what would have been Mike's birthday, I am feeling reflective.

The Queen Mother became a widow overnight at the age of 51; I became a widow with six years' warning, at the age of 54. She was a Queen; I'm a commoner. King George VI was around the same age as his wife; Mike was 19 years older than me. But we both became widows, regardless.

According to the programme I watched, a year after "Bertie's" death, The Queen Mother profoundly said, when asked how she was, "You don't get better; you get better *at* it."

I believe she was right.

I grieved twice for Mike: once, obviously, when he died, but I had already begun the process long before that, when I first lost the man I married to Alzheimer's. Even while Mike was still "alive", I carried a daily pain in my chest and a hollow feeling of loss throughout all my waking hours.

Those pains still come, the tears still flow, the wracking sobs still leave me exhausted, and my eyes and nose still get rubbed raw. However, I'm becoming much better at coping with my loss, feeling less cheated, and enjoying my memories. When Mike died, I carried memories with me, but they were of him during his illness. I'd almost forgotten the man he was before, the man I married, the man I'd loved for 30 years.

Now, I am reminded more and more often of our wonderful times, our special moments, our happy lives.

I will love Mike forever, and just writing those words makes the tears spill afresh, but I am getting better at being without him. I thank The Queen Mother for making me realise it.

My blog is still out there for anyone to stumble across, but I doubt that I will ever add to it, having now filled in the gaps and written this book. It's coming up to four years since Mike's death, and I still miss him. Every morning when I open the lounge curtains, I say hello to the photo I have of him, the one I had framed, especially for the funeral. It was one taken at the Eden Project when he was having a good day, and I will always remember the occasion with fondness. Obviously, I have lots of photos of him, mostly from before his illness, photos that document our thirty years together, photos that make me smile and remind me of the man I was lucky enough to meet and marry and raise a family with: my best friend; my love; my Mike.

Acknowledgements

If I tried to thank all those who helped me cope with Mike's Alzheimer's, the list would be endless. Suffice it to say that I am grateful for all the help and support that I got from family, friends and neighbours. Here, I will simply focus on the two people who helped me write this book.

The first is my daughter-in-law, Leah Spicer Pownall, who surprised me a few years ago by extracting all the blog posts and putting them in a Word document so that I could turn them into a book. This was extremely thoughtful and gave me the push I needed, although it took me time to get my act together.

I would also like to thank Phil Young, my long-time friend and neighbour, for creating my website and managing it over the years. There were times, like when I was at the hospital with Mike, that I would write a post on my phone and send it to Phil to upload for me.

Thank you, both.

Printed in Great Britain
by Amazon

22579801R00090